Building Hope

Bryan Parr

GO INTO ALL THE WORLD

AND WITNESS FOR THE LORD

EVEN USE WORDS IF YOU HAVE TO

Copyright April 2011 © Bryan Parr

Onwards and Upwards Publications
Berkeley House
11 Nightingale Crescent
West Horsley
Surrey
KT24 6PD
England

First Edition 2011

True Stories
www.onwardsandupwards.org

ISBN 978-1-907509-13-1

The right of Bryan Parr to be identified as the author of this work has been asserted by him in accordance with the Copyright, Designs and Patents Act 1988.

Cover design by Ana Marisa

All rights reserved.

No part of this publication may be reproduced or transmitted in any form or by any means, electronic or mechanical, including photocopy, recording or any information storage and retrieval system, without permission in writing from the author.

DEDICATION

To my wife Sylvia, for her patience, understanding and support over the 20 years of my travels.

Also to the good folk of Emmanuel Baptist Church who were generous in their support.

WARNING

Be careful what you ask of God as He is likely to answer your prayers as He did for me,

The result was many years of my life in service and travelling something like 80,000 miles, many overland.

YOU HAVE BEEN WARNED

Penryn to Tambov = 2500 miles
Penryn to Valca Crisului = 1600 miles
Penryn to Dezna = 1600 miles
Penryn to Brasov = 2000 miles

Moscow
Tambov
Penryn
Valca Crisului
Brasov
Dezna

My watch read 2.40am. It also told me that I was losing in my struggle to get a good night's sleep. I looked across the cab to see my wife Sylvia also struggling with the same problem, with little wonder considering the position she was in, her backside resting on our "Porta Potti", facing the cab roof, but with her head resting on the dashboard, her legs at a 90 degree angle up against the back of the cab. Not the most elegant posture, but the best that we could do under the circumstances. The non-stop rain that we had had to cope with, was still hammering down, now amplified by pounding away on the metal roof of our vehicle. Outside we were surrounded by twenty to thirty juggernauts, many with their engines running, supposedly to keep their refrigeration units going. The car park lights were on, and there was much coming and going, with the constant slamming of doors.

Once again I readjusted the pillow resting on the steering wheel, and tried to settle down, closing my eyes with the thought, "What are we doing here?" 'here' being Southern Germany en route to Romania. We had left our cosy little bungalow, and our king size bed in Penryn 48 hours earlier, and swapped it for this. For two people who share 130 years between us, the question had to be asked, "Are we mad?"

Not so; let me explain!

This journey started several years ago, in 1989. It was a Sunday evening, and I had spent my usual day in Church doing the usual things: singing, listening, and praying but, sadly, coming home feeling very dissatisfied. That evening I sat on my bed and asked God, "Is this it? Is **this** how my Christian walk will be for the rest of my earthly life?" Considering what I had been taught over the past few years, I was sure in my own mind that there just had to be more to the Christian life than what I was experiencing at that moment in time. So my prayer to God that night was that I would offer myself in service to Him and claim His promise that, "I will do whatever you ask in my name." (John 14 v 13) That said, I had no idea what to expect from God, but the frustration that was within me led me to believe that something would happen.

The very next day, I was informed that there was a meeting in Truro Baptist Church. It was Tuesday night and a man, a Russian man, recently released from a Soviet prison was there to give his testimony: a testimony about pain and suffering, the suffering coming about because he had proclaimed, "Jesus is Lord." Prior to President Gorbachev, Glasnost, and Perestroika, such a comment was all that it took to qualify for a five-year prison sentence. Such was the attitude of the Communists. Prison itself was not enough. It had to be isolation as well, so a prison thousands of miles away from friends, family, and Christian fellowship was where they sent you, and there they tried to break you. This man was one of the survivors of that regime. His faith had remained strong, and he was here to share with us what life was like living under the Communists. I left that meeting believing that I/we had no idea what real suffering was all about.

Under Communism, Bibles were not only not allowed, they were banned and, if found, destroyed. Those found in possession were in serious trouble, they and their families. This attitude was changing in the late 80s, early 90s, so much so that this was one of the pleas from our Russian brother: could we help with the sending of Bibles to our fellow believers in Russia? The facility for doing so was at hand; hence step two of my journey was taken!

The procedure was: one could buy X number of Bibles, 2 or 22, the more the better. You were given addresses and a green sticker which would get the package through customs unopened. Sadly, it cost more to post the Bibles than it did to buy them. A contact number was available to enable you to purchase more Bibles as and when one felt the prompting. With each package I sent off, I always put in a note of (hopefully) encouragement. This proved to be a wise move, as I began to receive letters of thanks from Russia.

God was at work!

That was the good news; the bad news was that I couldn't read them. What to do? Well, what I didn't do was to worry, because my God promised to meet my every need, so I passed it over to Him, and within a week I found myself sitting in the front room of a house in

Newquay, opposite a lady who hailed from what was Stalingrad. Naturally, she was fluent in all things Russian and gladly translated for me. Translation over, her curiosity got the better of her, and she wanted to know more about what was going on. After I had explained things to her, she actually broke down and cried, then expressed her gratitude to me, telling me of the desperate need for such literature in her country. I also found out that there was a small Russian fraternity in Cornwall, and this lady was able to put me in touch with another person who actually lived in Penryn. Her name was Tanya (more of Tanya later). The plot thickens!

One day, I received a letter from a man in Russia, written in English, expressing his gratitude and thanks for the gift of a Bible he had received and from that point on we began to correspond. His name was Gennadi, and Gennadi was a pastor of a Baptist Church in a very large town called Tambov.

Tambov is about 250 miles southeast of Moscow and has a population of about 300,000 people. We are now talking about a time in history when these people suddenly found themselves with religious freedom, so the cry for Christian literature was loud and strong. So I decided it would be best to send all the Bibles that I bought to Gennadi and trust his judgement as to whom he passed them on to. After corresponding with Gennadi over a period of several months, I wrote in one of my letters how wonderful it would be if he could come visit us in the U.K. In his return letter he stated that if I had mentioned such a thing in the past he would have been in serious trouble. Then, as it was, the timing of such a suggestion was fine. At this point it must be pointed out that these people were poor, in terms of finance, so to consider a trip from Tambov to Penryn would be a major undertaking - but the seed had been planted and had already started to grow.

God was at work!

After much correspondence had passed between us regarding this visit, and after a period of several weeks, Gennadi sent me a list of the people whom he thought would benefit most from such a visit: eight in all, three of whom were his church deacons, and another,

Tanya, who would be the interpreter. Again it must be mentioned that this was 1991 and the relationship between East and West was very strained with neither yet trusting the other and bureaucracy rampant. In seeking permission for applications to be successful, I must have written to every department in government. Assurances, insurances, guarantees, accommodation, health, motives, and reasons for such a visit, all had to be accounted for, with eight of us being accountable to eight of them. The paper work alone took several months before, what I felt, reluctant permission was granted.

I have to confess that near the end I was losing my patience, wondering: was this meant to be? One Sunday morning, I turned up at Emmanuel Baptist Church to be greeted by Sue Godfrey, our administrator, who handed me a letter from the Russian embassy stating that my applications had been accepted but could not be finalized unless it was all written out in the Russian language and returned a.s.a.p. That morning our minister, Michael Caddick, asked if there was anyone who would like prayer. I said, "Yes!" and went forward. After explaining about the letter and my frustration, Michael prayed, and after the prayer a stranger in the congregation stood up and said that she could read, write, and speak Russian, and was willing to help.

God was at work!

After the service was over, Sylvia and I took the lady home with us and, after lunch, set out all the paperwork, facts, figures, and personnel involved. She scooped everything up, ready to take it all home with her.(I had no idea where she lived). After a while she left, promising to do all that was necessary as soon as possible and would return it to me. Within the week, I had in my possession everything that I needed to put the finishing touches to what had to be done to satisfy the bureaucrats, both in this country and in Russia. This was a giant step forward for me, and at last I felt that it wasn't a case of one step forward and two steps back. By this time, Gennadi and I were communicating by phone, as well as letter, and he told me that things were just as difficult for him but that progress was being made. It's in situations like this that I remind myself that…

God doesn't ask us to be successful;
He asks us to be obedient.

And that...

it is not what we achieve that glorifies Him,
but what we overcome.

This meant believing that if we persisted with this struggle, and with the right attitude, then success would follow, and we would overcome, and this proved to be the case.

One evening, sat at home, the phone rang. It was Tanya, the interpreter, ringing me from Tambov. They were all ready to travel, she told me, and would be arriving at Heathrow at 10 am on a Thursday three weeks later. But, before she rang off, would I listen to something? Of course, I said, "Yes!" Then, from Tambov, deep in the heart of what was communist Russia came the sound of "Blessed Assurance" sung by Gennadi and the brothers, later asking, "Did it sound right?" and that they had learnt it especially to sing to us in Emmanuel. To me this was mind-boggling stuff. Twelve months earlier they would have been clapped in irons just for contemplating such a phone call. We had moved a long way in one year. Boundaries and cultures had been crossed, mountains had been climbed, and I...

praised the Lord!

I now had to make arrangements to hire a minibus, so it was off to Truro to have a chat with Vospers; sadly no concessions there, but we needed a quality vehicle with plenty of space. So I hired one of their 17-seaters for the weekend. Come the day, and it was off to Heathrow! There and back is too much for one man to do by himself in one day, so to share the driving Keith Jones, a fellow church member, agreed to come with me.

The journey up to Heathrow was uneventful and we had allowed ourselves plenty of time, arriving there by about 8.30pm. The reception area was very busy, with lots of people waiting for the flight to arrive. The plane landed on time but it was about 10.45 before any passengers made an appearance, and Gennadi and the others were the last to show.

We recognised each other immediately and instinctively, and after introductions all round, and after all had enjoyed a cool drink, I suggested that we pick up the luggage and make our way to the car park to start the long haul back to Cornwall.

Immediately they all formed a circle, and on cue, and without any inhibitions, they broke out into song. With their strong guttural voices they brought the reception area to a standstill. I didn't understand the words they sang but I felt quite sure that the other hundred or so passengers who came on the flight did, which made the whole episode a marvellous witness. I felt very excited, believing that this was going to be the start of something special. Again I thought:

God was at work!

Eventually we made it to the car park, loaded up the bus with the luggage and set off. Being aware that these people had left Tambov goodness-knows-how-many hours ago I asked if they would like to stop and have something to eat. With the answer being "Yes!" I pulled into a motorway service station. It was about 2.30 a.m. now, so the place was quite quiet with not too many people about. The place was well lit with lots of food on display, and straight away it became obvious that these good people felt uneasy and didn't know what to do.

"Bryan, is it okay if we take something?" they asked.

I grabbed a tray and led the way, telling them, "Help yourselves to whatever you want." (It wasn't until I visited Tambov myself that I realised how intimidating all this opulence was).

I led the way to the seating area where all the tables were set out to seat four people. This arrangement was not acceptable.

"We are family," they said, "and we fellowship together," so after a hasty rearrangement of furniture, and when all were sat down, another chorus was sung by all, followed by a short prayer. Only then did we eat!

Eating over, and back on the road, lots of questions were asked, one of which was, "Will we see the sea?"

I explained that Cornwall is surrounded by water, but couldn't understand why they would ask such a question. Later I learned that Tambov is in the middle of Russia, and being land-locked meant that these people had never left home before and had never seen such an ocean of water, so seeing the Atlantic was going to be a new experience for them. Hence the excitement and another lesson to be learned by me!

We arrived in Cornwall during the early hours of the morning, and after dropping each off at their respective hosts, I went home to catch up on my 'beauty sleep'. For a while I just lay in my bed and thought about all that had happened: all the phone calls, the letter writing, the frustrations, the encouragement and the prayer. Difficult as it had been, just meeting these people made it all worthwhile, and I knew in my heart that there was a lot more to come. Because of the long journey from Tambov, I told everyone involved that nothing was planned for the first 24 hours. All could rest for a while, and then we would all meet at Emmanuel Baptist Church. I fell asleep, feeling good and knowing that…

God was at work!

Gennadi, being a Baptist minister, was naturally interested in not only the buildings but also the way we did things, hence the many conversations with Michael, our minister. I felt sure that this was quality time for both men. Many of Emmanuel Church's members took a great interest in these, our brothers from far away. Much hospitality was forthcoming and many evenings spent in different homes. During the daytime, trips to other "places of worship" were high on the agenda: Truro Cathedral was of special interest; Lands End, with the ocean beyond, fascinated them; eating pasties in Falmouth, followed by a civic reception in the Mayor's office. Their photographs, taken with an English 'bobby', made the local press, and a tasty Sunday lunch in The Green Lawns Hotel went down well with all concerned.

Waiting for lunch to be served, I was asked why we needed so much cutlery. I tried to explain, but they just said, *"Bryan you have too much."*

I must confess I found it hard to disagree with them. For the ten days spent in Cornwall God saw fit to bless us with warm sunny days, of which we took full advantage, with many an exhausting walk and lots of sightseeing. During a conversation with Tanya, she explained about the trials and tribulations they all went through to make the journey possible, not least of which was the finance, and how their fellowship had rallied around and supported them throughout. It seems that they were quoted a price for the party to travel by air and, arriving at the airport with the right amount for their tickets, were shattered when told that the price had gone up.

Tanya explained that some time ago Gennadi had taken into their fellowship a convicted criminal and a habitual drunkard. They had nurtured and cared for this man over a period of time, and wanting to show his appreciation for what 'the church' had done for him, he had volunteered to drive the bus with all on board from Tambov to Moscow airport. This man now volunteered to return to Tambov and raise the extra cash needed for the tickets. Gennadi agreed but was concerned about this man's past and the temptation which would come his way, being trusted with this much needed money. Also the fact that they could all be stuck in Moscow, without transport, should he give in to temptation. One can only assume that the Christian love shown to this man had had the desired effect, because he returned with the necessary funds for the tickets to be paid for. Once again, their fellowship rallying to the cause, coupled with this man's honesty shining through, gave cause for a double celebration.

The members of Emmanuel Church rallied around these brothers and sister, so much so that we were able to take them shopping for much needed underwear, socks, shoes, etc., for which they were all extremely grateful. Ten days passed very quickly, probably because so much was packed into each day; so many people to see and so many places to go. On the penultimate night a grand farewell meal was held in Emmanuel. This was not only to show corporate hospitality but for individuals to say farewell. Arrangements had been made with another fellowship in the London area to host these people for three or four days, to enable them to see a few of the sites in London. So I drove them to a service station at Fleet on the A303 and safely handed them over. Once again it was an emotional time for all concerned as we said our farewells, but I left them with the promise that one day I would make the journey to Tambov so that we could all meet up again.

Everyone wanted this relationship to develop even further. And so I returned home and reflected on all that had taken place to bring about what I considered to be a momentous chapter in my journey. Little did I know that the best was yet to come! But before that, a lot more planning, letter writing, telephoning and praying had to be done, and having climbed one mountain, I could start climbing the next one with confidence, because I just knew that…

God was at work!

IF ONE’S FAITH IS NOT SACRIFICIAL

YOU HAVE TO QUESTION ITS VALUE

TAMBOV

The beginning of part two of this journey started off much the same as part one: lots of paper work and forward planning. The second time round some of it became easier because of earlier experience, but this was counter-balanced by the fact that now we were doing the travelling, which meant a completely different set of documents.

I had let it be known in the church 'fellowship' that this mission was in the planning and, should anyone be interested, to let me know. Lots of people declared an interest initially, but for various and legitimate reasons many had to back out. Eventually the team consisted of eight people: John and Sylvia Allenach, Jean Frazier, Phil and Sue Misselbrook, Peter Curgenven, Sylvia and myself. Costs were worked out for various modes of transport, with us eventually settling for the train. This proved to be a wise choice as we eventually finished up with a great deal of luggage, which we wouldn't have been able to take with us by any other means of transport.

As with all things, finance plays a big part, so we immediately started fund-raising. This was a responsibility shared by everyone, as the costs involved were considerable. Again Emmanuel got behind us and showed their support by attending the dinners that were organised. We had donations given, we held car-boot sales and table top sales, we raised and sold plants: whatever we could think of that would swell the coffers! This activity went on until our target was reached.

Running parallel to the fund raising was the paper work that was needed for the dreaded bureaucrats, only now it was a little more trying because something new was added. We were having to travel across Poland, so now I had England, Russia, and Poland to deal with, but with perseverance being the name of the game, eventually all things slotted into place.

By now the team was meeting on a regular basis, each contributing different ideas. It was during one such meeting that we brought Tanya on board. You recall that I first got to know about Tanya during the early stages of this journey, she being a part of the

Russian fraternity in Cornwall. This lady was proving to be an important piece of this jigsaw!

The team had decided that it would show itself willing and create a good impression if we learned some choruses in the Russian language, plus one or two other phrases that we thought might be useful. For instance, "Where is the toilet?" was high on everyone's list, and Tanya agreed to be our teacher. So, in addition to everything else, now we had weekly lessons in the Russian language to contend with, and added to that, Sylvia and John had decided to learn a prayer in Russian. All very impressive but all very worthwhile as we were to learn much later. Our enthusiasm meant that we were good pupils, and we learnt well and quickly.

As stated earlier, this journey started with the purchasing of Bibles some 18 months previous and it was decided that we would buy some more Christian literature to take with us. So I made contact with the suppliers, an organisation called A.R.C. (Aid to Russian Christians). The Bibles were bought, paid for, and packed away in readiness for our departure. A few weeks later a letter arrived from A.R.C. asking me to pay my bill. This puzzled me as I always pay for whatever by return of post, and my bank statement showed evidence of this, so I rang them to clarify the situation.

They asked, "Are you Bryan Parr?"

I said, "Yes!"

They asked, "Did you recently buy some Bibles?"

I said, "Yes!"

They said, "And you live in Chester."

And I said, "No!"

Problem solved! They had got their wires crossed, and although I didn't know it at the time, this was to be another piece of the jigsaw slotting into place and one more blessing.

Apparently there were two Bryan Parr's and both doing the same kind of work. I asked them to give me the telephone number of the Bryan Parr in Chester, which they did. I made contact with this man, and it soon became apparent that our paths were meant to cross. Not only did we share the same name, he also was a Christian man and, as stated, doing the same kind of work. In addition, he had his own printing press and was turning out tracts, gospels, and calendars, all printed in the Russian Language, and for no charge he would send me as many of these publications as I wanted. This, I believe, was a heaven-sent opportunity and too good to miss. I asked for, and received, 300 calendars, 2000 tracts and 100 Gospels.

Praise the Lord!

Although there was no charge levied for this literature, I considered it appropriate to make a contribution to the costs involved so that everyone would benefit through mutual support. This duly happened! It was during our conversation, that Bryan said that he had only ever seen one other person with the name 'Parr', and that was on a builder's van that that he saw on a regular basis driving around the streets of Chester. It occurred to me that this must be my long-lost brother. My moving south several years earlier and he roaming Portugal and Spain in a motor home for several years meant that we had lost touch. Now with this sighting, I realised that he may be back in circulation in what was his home town of Chester, so I suggested to Bryan that the next time he spotted the van, he should stop it, give the driver (providing it was my brother David) my telephone number and ask him to make contact. This in fact did take place, and my brother and I were reunited and in regular contact with each other. One more piece of the jigsaw slotted in.

God was at work!

Time was moving along swiftly now, departure date coming up fast, finance in place, ferry crossing had been booked, train tickets purchased and compulsory sleeping berths all booked and confirmed. And with the dubious renditions of 'God's not Dead', 'Come into His Presence' and 'Bind us Together, Lord' in the Russian language learned and fixed in our minds, we felt that we were ready for our epic journey into the unknown. Each of us felt assured that our God had gone before us and had already paved the way. We were all in high spirits and eager to be off.

With all the frustrations now behind me I felt that I could relax a little whilst not allowing complacency to set in. It is fortunate that I check and double-check things, because only two weeks before departure date, I found out that the travel agent hadn't received our visas to pass through Poland. He didn't even realise that we needed them. I felt somewhat annoyed that I had to tell him something that he should have already known. Thankfully the visas arrived in time, so all was well. In putting this whole mission together, mountains had been climbed and much had been overcome. I do feel a certain satisfaction here. I also believe that I could not have got this far without the good Lord supporting me.

The day dawned, Tuesday 9th of June 1992, and the team agreed to meet at my place at 21.45 hours. The bus had been loaded during the afternoon, so it was now a time for prayer, to ask God's blessing on each of us. The journey was in excess of 3000 miles each way, travelling across southern England, Belgium, Germany, Poland, then into Russia. Moscow was where we disembarked from the train, then travelled by bus to Tambov, another 250 miles. We certainly needed 'travelling mercies'.

Prayer time was over, and people started to arrive to see us off: Michael, our minister, and his wife, Elizabeth, Tracy Rogers and her two daughters, Michelle and Sarah, Peter's wife, Gill, and his son Simon. So at 10.15 pm. we started our journey.

As is usual on such a trip, at the beginning there is a lot of chatter and banter, but because of the lateness of the hour, heads soon began to nod. Thankfully Phil Ferris, our driver, was not one of them, so we kept a steady course for Dover. We had allowed plenty of time so that there was no need to go too fast, our safety being paramount.

We arrived safely at Dover at 6am, tired but still in high spirits. The boat, the Prince Albert, didn't leave until 9am, which gave us plenty of time to have a wash and brush up, then have an early breakfast, find a large trolley for our considerable luggage and make our way to the boarding area. Travelling overnight in the bus meant that we had had little sleep.

All safely on board, it was cast-off time, and sharp on nine o'clock we set sail on our six hour crossing, heading for the port of Oostende in Belgium. Thankfully the crossing was smooth, and no one was poorly. It was a short step from the ship to the railway station, where once again we commandeered a large trolley for our luggage. We had a three hour wait for the train, but apparently this time was not to be wasted. God was at work and another piece of the jigsaw was about to be slotted into place.

On the platform, waiting for the same train as us, was an elderly couple. The man, Theodore, was from the Ukraine and 48 years before had escaped from his hometown because of the communist persecution. To escape to the West was considered a major crime, which would have had serious repercussions if he had been caught. Now many years later, he and his English wife had decided to return. Because of this man's age he felt a great desire to return and see the family that he had left behind all those years ago. But he was afraid. His fear was that the communists could have long memories, and would they be waiting for him? It was the unknown that was causing his concern.

We spent some time with this couple, hopefully reassuring them, praying with them and for them. I do believe that they gained some peace of mind. Our time spent waiting for the train was not wasted.

God was at work!

It was during this waiting time that I spoke to one of the railway officials about out departure time and was quite alarmed to be told that the train would leave about two minutes after its arrival, which did not give us too much time to get on board considering our amount of luggage etc. Giving this some thought, I suggested that all the ladies just got on board and grabbed a seat. John and Phil should climb aboard and grab the entire luggage as Peter and I piled it through the door. Once on our way we could sort it all out at our leisure. This proved to be a wise decision and a hectic two minutes followed. Once on our way, we started to get ourselves in order. There were three sleeping bunks per compartment, so we decided who would sleep in each. That sorted, we were able to sort out our luggage.

When we had left home on Tuesday, we knew that we had a very long journey ahead of us and, as we were going into the unknown, had no idea what lay ahead. So we tried to think of everything that we would need for our personal comfort. That meant a part of our luggage was made up of food. Sandwiches were eaten first. Then it was down to tinned stuff: cracker biscuits and fruit. I don't know if it was the same throughout the train, but we had an attendant for our carriage to whom we introduced ourselves and established a good relationship. His name was Georgi, but he soon learned to answer to 'George'. His home was in Moscow. We got to know him quite well by the end of our journey. As stated earlier, this was the month of June, and it was proving to be a hot one, so we soon learned that a steady liquid intake was going to be necessary; hence we encouraged 'George' to keep the kettle on the boil, which meant that we had a steady supply of "chie" (tea).

I, personally, have to confess to a childlike excitement about this whole mission. Therefore, I spent many hours standing in the passage, looking out of the window. The scenery was ever changing as we left the more civilised world of the West behind us and travelled East into what was a much poorer environment. The big industries, towns and cities of Germany gave way to much more rural communities. There was much more open land, which was being cultivated by the locals, with lots of small allotments and people using scythes and other hand tools. There was less motorised movement, more horses and carts, and the people themselves looked more peasant-like, with many a small child helping out with the work. As we sped by, they looked up and waved.

As this part of the world was very much underdeveloped, it meant that it had retained much of its natural beauty. Many a forest and lake passed by, with everything blending in together, making for some spectacular views. All this in turn helped to keep our interest alive as we whizzed along at a fair lick, covering many a mile in a short space of time and many a spool of film being used up.

Things usually started to happen at about 7am, not all rising at the same time. Sharing the same sleeping quarters meant that some discretion had to be used, plus the fact that there was only one loo, and that was used by other passengers as well as us. We soon discovered that it was wise to let Sylvia go first as she took a rag and disinfectant with her. After that we all thought, "Now it's safe!" and formed an orderly queue in the corridor, whilst Sue made the beds.

After our wash and brush up it was time for breakfast: cracker biscuits, cheese, fruit and 'chie'. Then it was a Bible reading and prayer time. That done, it was back into the corridor to look out of the window again.

By now we were well into Poland and the environmental change was even more marked: little or no industry at all, and the horse seemed to be the main source of transport. Eastern Poland and Western Russia seemed to be one enormous allotment, with man, woman, and child tending the land from dawn till dusk. They were very industrious people, the industry perhaps born out of necessity. (Such was my understanding.)

After a while our tummies told us it was lunchtime. We tried to vary our diet, so this time we had a tin of beans with our fruit and 'chie'. During the journey Theodore was not neglected. We had many a chat with him and his wife and gave him a gospel as a parting gift.

Our first stop was Warsaw and this was where Theodore left us, but before he went we invited him into our compartment and prayed with him. He cried, told of his appreciation for our prayers and care, then left. We never saw him again.

About 150/160 miles further on from Warsaw we arrived at Brest, which is on the Polish/Russian border. Here we had the experience of having the whole train lifted about six feet into the air. This was in order to have a different set of wheels put on, as the gauge of track is different in Russia. Security was tight, and no one was allowed off the train whilst this was going on. Suspicion and security is a by-word here. That done, we moved from the sheds to the station, and this was where the police and customs moved in. They were a stern looking bunch: all were armed and knew their business! They searched our luggage and eventually gave us a clean bill of health.

They still asked a lot of questions, wanting to know why we were visiting Russia, where we would be staying and for how long. Jean had a lot of explaining to do, as in their opinion she was carrying a lot of money and they actually marched her off to clarify things to the officer in charge. The whole experience was a bit daunting, but necessary I suppose, and as all our paperwork was in order, everything eventually proved to be acceptable to them. Not so with other passengers in our carriage. These were Polish nationals and were given a hard time by these officials, emptying their suitcases unceremoniously, bullying, and generally intimidating them.

History tells us that there is not much love lost between these two nations and it certainly showed in this instance. Whatever the outcome of all this, eventually it was all over. We all relaxed and started on our way once more.

Once on our way, it immediately became obvious that this driver was in one heck of a hurry. I personally don't think that the wheels touched the track and at times thought we were airborne.

We had been travelling for more than 60 hours now and had covered more than 3000 miles. Although we had our bunks to sleep in, none of us was actually getting a good night's sleep. It was very hot and dry, so we were drinking as much water and 'chie' as possible. Liquid was more important than food as we needed to prevent dehydration, and although we were all insured, we still needed to take all the precautions that were necessary to safeguard our well-being.

We were fast approaching Moscow now and I asked George, "What is our E.T.A (estimated time of arrival)?"

The answer was "15.10" and at precisely 15.10 we rolled into Moscow station. Eat your heart out B.R!

Tremendous excitement now emerged with lots of hugs and kisses. The reception committee was there: Pastor Gennadi, two of his three sons, Volodiya and Eugenie, Pavel, and Pasha, two of Gennadi's deacons, Tanya, the interpreter, and Lem and Vera from Penryn (Tanya's mum and dad).

After sorting our luggage we were escorted to two dubious-looking vehicles into which we loaded it all. Then we set off for Tambov, another eight hours of travelling. The team was very tired but still in high spirits. The first thing that became obvious was that this was not going to be a smooth ride. The roads were very bad, and we had only gone about three miles when we unsurprisingly had a puncture. We all piled out of the bus to enable Pavel to affect a repair. My heart sank a little when he opened up the back compartment of the bus and selected what was the best of about six bald tyres. With repairs done, and back on the road, we realised that we had lost contact with the other vehicle. So we turned around to go and find them. That's when we got another puncture.

Same repair procedure and we were off again. We found the others. They too had broken down. Their problem was mechanical. It seems that this must be a way of life for these people, as they seem to carry a variety of spares and are prepared for almost anything that may happen. At this point the team decided that some prayer was essential, not only for our safety but to actually get us there. The prayer was answered, because we had a trouble-free drive from that point on, eventually arriving in Tambov at 2am on the Saturday. Each of us was dropped off at our respective host's, very tired, and glad to have arrived safely; Tuesday night 10pm until 2am Saturday morning, virtually non-stop travelling. That was some journey!

Excitement and enthusiasm were still running high, and despite our tiredness we were all up and about by about 10 am on the following day. We had an easy day, but we were gearing ourselves up for an evening service in Pastor Gennadi's church, a service in which we were to play a major part. Apart from our personal luggage, we had brought a great deal of other merchandise with us, from Bibles to needles and cotton, so we spent the day unpacking and sharing things with these good people. Zina, Gennadi's wife immediately went for the needle and cotton and a card of buttons. That act alone was significant to me, and served to increase my desire to know more about these people, and their way of life.

The day went well, and the informal fellowship was good, spending a lot of time around a 'samovar', a very decorative teapot with little cups hanging from it. This was placed in the middle of the table, and many people throughout the day just popped in, helped themselves to 'chie', and chatted. They wanted to know about us, and we wanted to know about them.

Evening arrived, and it was time to go to church. During the early part of the year, when this mission was in the organising stage, it was decided that we would make some banners to take with us. This fell in the lap of Sue, and the result was first class. Our theme was 'Bind us together Lord', so Sue had produced a magnificent banner proclaiming just that, written in both English and Russian. It showed people of different colour and race, all holding hands, and surrounding a globe that represented the world. It was at the service that night that we intended to present these banners, three in total.

The church was full that night, which was very encouraging. The informal service was handed over to us to conduct as we felt right but always under the authority of Gennadi. Bryan led the proceedings, explaining why we had come and the background to the whole mission. Phil brought 'the Word' and received a good response. Peter and Bryan presented the banners to lots of 'ooo's and 'aah's. John and Sylvia closed proceedings with a prayer in Russian. All this was mingled with our renditions of 'Bind us together Lord', 'God's not Dead', and 'Come into His Presence', all in Russian; from their reaction, they were quite impressed.

We also took lots of goodies for the children, so after the service was over, Sylvia and Jean shared these gifts; that done, we all retired to a room in the rear and shared a meal together.

This was early days, but we learned later that these people had been saving food for some considerable time in order that we wouldn't go hungry. Throughout our stay with these brothers and sisters, our food intake was mainly potatoes, eggs, chicken, salad stuff and bread. All this produce was home grown and all was greatly appreciated. At 9.30pm we went to our homes, all quite tired; it was still Saturday, and as yet we had not fully recovered from the journey. By ten o'clock we were all in bed and asleep.

Sunday morning: another service in Pastor Gennadi's church, and again we were to play a major part. There were lots of new faces in the congregation, and again the place was full, with some people having to stand at the rear.

I again led the proceedings, and Phil again brought 'the Word'. Peter gave his testimony and Sylvia Allanach said the prayers. We rededicated the banners, and they were hung in what was to be their permanent positions.

To our embarrassment and delight, we were asked to sing our songs again, which of course we did, except that when we sang 'Bind us Together', we moved amongst them and held hands. This was something new to them but something that they accepted and responded to. I believe that that act took away any inhibitions that may have been lingering between us. After the service there was a very relaxed atmosphere, lots of chat, questions being asked from both sides, addresses exchanged, and new friendships formed. It was greatly encouraging!

We were advised to rest in the afternoon, and to be ready to take a service in a large auditorium that same night. Gennadi said that there might be up to a thousand people there, mostly non-believers, people that he had been preaching to for a long time, and he was praying that our presence might make a difference and a breakthrough.

This was a very big challenge for us; I personally had never spoken publicly on such a scale. But each of us felt that it was God at work and that He would enable us. We covered ourselves in prayer, asking for courage and boldness.

We persisted with our theme 'Bind us Together', again using the banner as a visual aid. At the end of the service we gave out the challenge to the congregation to come to repentance; the response was tremendous, with all the team taking up the opportunity to minister to these people. It was here that we relied on Gennadi and his members to help us with translation. The whole evening was highly successful, and Gennadi told me later that we had had a profound effect on these people with our direct approach to the Gospel, plus the fact that we were prepared to come all the way from Cornwall to tell of God's love. That meant a great deal to them. We also encouraged these people to make personal contact with Gennadi, to enable further development to take place. Our prayers had been answered!

After the service was over, a video showing the crucifixion was shown on the large screen; I was assured that it made a big impact on all present. After that, we all went out into the foyer, where Gennadi had set up tables and was distributing all the tracts, gospels, calendars that we had brought with us. This again prompted very fruitful conversation. This whole day had been tremendous, and we, as a team, believed that if this was going to be a typical day, we were only now beginning to realize how God was going to use us. We got back to our homes about 10 pm, had a light supper and so to bed.

On Monday we were told that it was essential that we reported to the area visa office to get our passports stamped, which in turn gave us the official permission to be in Tambov. Failure to do so would mean that the police would come looking for us, and we didn't want that. To get there we took the local tram (quite an experience - fast and bumpy!) The officials were happy with our paper work, which meant that we got the necessary stamp of approval. All that attention to detail during the planning was now paying off.

This was to be a kind of rest day for us, so whilst in the city we went on a sight-seeing tour. Tambov is a city approximately 350 years old and has a population of about 300,000 people. Sadly it has a distinctly run-down appearance, roads that we in England would consider positively dangerous. It was very dusty and very, very hot. We visited museums, a music academy, the former K.G.B. headquarters (which was now a wedding chapel), Lenin square and the local park; there are statues and reminders of Lenin everywhere. It is also a city that is very proud of its war record; it was a place where tanks were mass-produced, and the Russian T34 was one of the best tanks made during W.W.2. It also boasted of a female battalion of soldiers; they too covered themselves with glory. It was during this walkabout that we met Seth. He was English, a retired minister. His wife had died not too long ago, and rather than sit at home, he had decided to do a tour of this region. Sadly, he wasn't feeling well, and he did not have any medication. So we suggested that he spent some time with us, which he gladly accepted.

When we got back to Gennadi's, we looked in the medicine kit we had brought with us, and we had just the medication Seth needed.

God was at work.

Late afternoon, and we all gathered at Pastor Gennadi's house where we shared a meal together. There followed a time of spontaneous worship which helped set us up for another service that night in Pastor Gennadi's church.

Again we were asked to minister to the fellowship, which had now become much easier for us, as we felt that we were among friends. This would be the last time that we would see these people so we wanted to be among them. I again led proceedings and addressed the congregation; then each of the team spoke, expressing their heart-felt feelings and what all this had meant to them. We were asked to sing some English choruses, so we finished with what was our anthem: 'Bind us Together Lord'. Another tremendous day!

The next day we started off quite leisurely. Wanting to see more of this part of the world we decided on a boat trip. There were sixteen of us and we actually hired a steamer all to ourselves and at very little cost. We travelled down the river Sna on another very hot day. Many parts of the river were completely covered with lilies, which added to the interest and beauty. We landed on a small island and went walking, but we were soon glad to get back on board and relax under the canopy, getting some respite from the relentless sun.

The heat was exceptional. We were conscious of dehydration so we drank as much as possible, mostly water. That presented another problem; it was not quite as pure as we would have liked it to have been. It was the lesser of two evils. These were the things we had to overcome. We felt that it was essential to continue to cover ourselves with prayer.

We tried to be in bed at a respectable time, getting as much rest as possible as the heat was taking its toll. In the meantime Gennadi's two sons, Eugenie and Gennadi Jnr. had been at work in the garden and had made up a wooden frame with draped plastic around it and a water container on top. From the container came a short length of hose pipe with a watering can rose clipped on the end. They then carried buckets of water from the house and filled up the container, and *hey presto*, a shower. Believe me, crude and rough as this shower was, it got a five star rating from all that used it. It also illustrated how concerned they were for our well-being. And so, rested and showered, we got ready for our next challenge. We were to visit a youth club in town. Peter took charge of the night's program; there were about sixty children present. There was singing, testimony, and Phil and Sue did a drama. We ended up by getting all the children to sing, "Our God is so good, so strong and so mighty" with all the actions, naturally. We also had some treats for these children, which were well received. Everyone enjoyed themselves, and Gennadi said that we had made a good impression and that he was well pleased.

Wednesday was shopping day. We needed something to take back with us that would remind us of what I believed to be a momentous experience. I think that we were all impressed with our 'samovars', which came in various sizes and were very decorative. They have a practical everyday use. but I suspect that ours will be more ornamental. From the gift shops we went to the market place: a bad move. It was a dreadful place; hygiene was non-existent, the place was dirty and the smell terrible. There were hundreds of people picking things up, smelling them, then putting them back. I came upon a bench with a cow's head on display, its tongue hanging out, eyes still in, horns still on, and what seemed like a million flies covering it. I had had enough; I didn't mind sampling local culture, but I was only prepared to go so far. I felt upset that people had to buy such 'fare', and that this was normal everyday life for them. I went and sat in the bus, waiting for the others to come out. (They weren't too long in coming).

We had a meal at Tolyer's house, one of Gennadi's deacons. It was a sumptuous meal, the same menu but with different faces present, but sadly this occasion was tinged with sadness. Some of these people belonged to a second Baptist church in this area of Tambov, and there was a gulf between the two congregations. Gennadi's wanted to reach out to the community; the other was reluctant to follow that route because of the fear of contamination. They talked to each other and respected each other but, with different ideologies, seldom mixed.

That day I could sense a difference in the team. The strain was beginning to show. I think the heat was the problem. We were just not getting enough liquid inside us. We had been practising boiling the water before drinking, then letting it go cold, but we didn't have access to that much, so we were drying out.

In the afternoon we were meant to set out for Murschansk, about a hundred kilometres away. Sylvia was not at all well; and travelling that far, mid afternoon, with such heat, on dusty and bumpy roads, in a not too comfortable bus, I thought it would be best that she would stay behind in the cool. With access to plenty of cool liquid and a rest, I felt sure she would be fine. We set off for an evening service, so the timing and distance meant it was going to be a long day, which made me all the more glad that Sylvia was not with us. On arrival there was some animated talk between our hosts and Gennadi. It seemed that the local communist chief (they still had some influence locally) had forbidden us the use of the hall that we were going to use, but undaunted, these people had plan B ready.

Driving another mile or two, we left the road and set off across country. We came to what looked like a couple of barns, which were enclosed by a six foot fence. Two large doors swung open and we went into a court yard; 25 to 30 people were there waiting for us, and we received a warm and friendly greeting, though I must admit that everyone felt a bit awkward at first. Once again language proved to be the stumbling block, but it didn't take long before all inhibitions were swept aside, everybody relaxed, and the chat flowed freely, even though we couldn't understand much of it. Again we broke into song and they reciprocated. Phil and Sue did some drama, and again Peter gave his testimony. All this interaction went a long way to setting the tone of the evening, being relaxed and enjoyable. Although we didn't realise it at the time, there was quite a feast being prepared for us. These people really blessed us in so many ways. Their singing is different from ours; they seem to have a "guttural" sound that comes from deep down and comes out vibrant, strong, and resonant, whereas ours comes from the mouth and sounds quite different.

The room where we ate was laid out with very simple wooden benches and tables. They sat one side, and we sat opposite; thus we each had someone to talk to. I noticed on the end wall that there was a simple wooden cross, just two pieces of 4x2 nailed together and hung on two nails: very simple and very poignant. Many tales were told that night, and I found myself being very impressed by them. It was only from some of these stories that I begin to realise how evil communism was, and it was a tribute to these people's faith that they survived such oppression. I was finding the whole experience something very special.

Peter was especially pleased to meet some of these brothers who were the local firemen, as Peter was from Penryn, so after the meal and fellowship, it was down to the local fire-station where Peter was given a conducted but brief tour of the station. This made for an even better end to Peter's day, although for him the best was yet to come.

Before we left, we learned that the local population had organised a demonstration to take place, with the intention of removing the local bureaucrats who were still practising communism.

That done, a democratic election would take place - something that had never happened in their lifetime before! We wished them well.

Service over, lots of hugs and kisses, goodbyes said and it was back on board the bus, where we were off on our return trip to Tambov. It was a hot sticky night and it was late when we arrived. We were all ready for our beds! Sylvia was waiting for me. Having a day off had proved to be a wise decision. She felt a lot better, which pleased and relieved me. It has been an eventful, day, and a day that I would cherish.

God had been at work again!

A casual day was planned next with the early part spent sight-seeing and a bit more shopping. In the late afternoon we had a twenty mile drive to a village called Razzkazova to lead another service. Seth felt that it was time for him to carry on with his journey. We agreed, and as we were all going to town sightseeing and shopping, we thought it right and proper to take him to the station and see him off. With Seth vanishing over the horizon, we headed for town. It was during our walkabout that we came across the local fire station. Due to Peter's interest, we boldly entered and Peter introduced himself. There were about six or seven men on duty with the station officer.

They made us very welcome, and Peter was given a conducted tour of the station and a demonstration of the appliances. We spent the best part of an hour with them, and much to Peter's delight, when it was time to go, they presented to him a book of photographs, showing their fire-fighting experiences and many of the big fires that they had attended in and around the Tambov region - a superb book, in colour and signed by all the firemen. Peter treasures that book to this day!

At this stage, Igor joined our team. Igor was a young man and a highly trained micro-surgeon, specialising in eye surgery. Once again, I was totally perplexed by this culture. Igor was so poorly paid (£18 per month) that he had to go from Tambov to Moscow each weekend so that he could earn some extra money, showing tourists around the capital. Igor spoke very good English. He spent a couple of days with us and was a tremendous help with the language problem. Wherever we went we had tracts with us, which we distributed liberally.

When Igor suggested that we pay a visit to the hospital where he worked, it was thought that it would be a good place to witness and use our literature. This visit again proved to be quite an eye-opener. On arrival at the hospital, we entered a small reception area, where we had to remove our shoes and cover our feet with plastic bags. We then went through into the main reception area, where Igor greeted us and proceeded to give us a conducted tour. The interior of this place was second to none, immaculately clean, with all the latest equipment. It was very impressive. Igor, being a specialist in eye surgery, showed us where he worked, and it was fascinating.

A carousel unit was set up in the middle of the room, circular in shape, and accommodating eight beds. All the patients' feet pointed to the centre, and obviously all the heads were on the outer edge. Eight doctors sat on eight seats and attended an individual patient. Each doctor had a specific task; that done, the carousel was moved round one place and the next doctor performed his task. By the time the unit had reached doctor number eight, all he had to do was bandage the patient's eye and then they were free to go. Igor said that operating this way they got through all their patients in quick time and did not have a waiting list. I have been told that this method had been tried in England but was rejected. We spoke to some of the people there about our faith and gave out tracts and gospels to many people. Wherever we went, we were witnessing and evangelising.

That day we ate with Pasha, one of Gennadi's deacons. Pasha was a concern. He worked very hard for his church, he had a day job, and because his wife suffered from depression, he cared not only for her but for the two children as well. Thankfully, he was a resilient character with a strong faith and with good support from his fellowship. All this made Pasha a survivor. One of the many things that I have learnt here is that although these people may be poor in terms of money and materials, they are rich in community spirit and quite willing to meet each other's needs. It's probably easy for me to philosophise, but I could well imagine this community spirit being the result of the communist way of life. It perhaps made this attitude a necessity, and the need to help one another became a way of life.

It was late afternoon now, and we had to get ready for our drive to Razzkazova. This fellowship proved to be something that you could call ‘different’ - a ‘throwback’ to the ‘old’ days when people had to meet in someone’s home because of the oppression. That is exactly what this was, an ordinary home, but now a church to this little community of people. The lounge was the place of worship and fellowship. The seating, to accommodate about thirty people maximum, was arranged with a small raised platform for a speaker. I estimate the room size to be no more than fifteen feet by twenty feet, and it was full. Not only were they in full voice but it was a joyful sound too.

Peter was responsible for the evening program, and after receiving a warm welcome, we clamped shoulder to shoulder because of the lack of space and gave forth our renditions in Russian. John spoke to the people that night and said the closing prayer in Russian. Everywhere we went we gave the challenge for repentance, but tonight was different. Everyone was already fully committed. I felt it to be impossible to put into words the feeling, atmosphere and warmth one experienced from these gatherings. These people were dedicated, sincere, and reverent. Their appreciation of us, what we were doing, how far we had travelled, was clearly shown by the many tears that were shed when it came to the time for our departure. We left for Tambov at 9.30pm, which meant another ‘hairy’ drive and the customary puncture. It was quite late when we got back home, and we didn’t need much encouragement to go to bed. We were cramming so much into each day and we were tired, but there was just so much to do and see, and nobody knew if we would ever pass that way again. Again that day I felt truly blessed, and I just knew that…

God had been at work.

Friday, and this was really intended to be a day of leisurely activities. That night we planned to set off for Moscow, but first had piled into a bus, and armed with our swimming trunks and costumes, we had set off to see some of the local countryside and have a swim in the local river. The weather was still very hot and humid, so we did not have much energy. It was at bit cooler by the river, which was a welcome relief. Some of us, however, still had enough energy to take a stroll in the woods, but mostly we just took things easy.

Early afternoon and we all had lunch with Pastor Gennadi and his family, plus a few friends. This was followed by some singing, a short discussion from the Bible and a time when we each voiced our thanks and appreciation for all that we had seen and done, and what the whole experience had meant to each of us.

After that, each of us had to go to our respective homes, start packing, and get ready for the trip to Moscow. We had decided to travel to Moscow by train. The cost was negligible, and anything was going to be better than the buses that we had been using. We left Tambov station at 8.50pm, with Pasha and Eugenie keeping pace with the train until they ran out of platform. Tanya and one or two of the brothers came with us, all of whom could speak some English, which was essential for our general well-being. Although we had left Tambov behind, it was by no means the end of our time in Russia.

We arrived in Moscow at 6am on the Saturday, and after leaving the train, we headed for the metro. Travelling was much easier now, as we had left a great deal of our luggage behind. When visiting Moscow, we were encouraged to travel on the metro. It's a system that the Muscovites were mightily proud of, and rightly so. There was polished marble everywhere, chandeliers for lighting, gargoyles, displays, statues, and tributes to Lenin all around. The trains were fast and frequent, and one had to know exactly what to do. No hanging about; time and the metro wait for no man. Our underground journey took us about an hour. We were actually heading for Lev and Vera's home on the outskirts of the city. Lev and Vera were the parents of 'Penryn Tanya', and they had quite a large apartment, which could accommodate most of the team. The others were to stay in Tanya's flat, which was about a fifteen-minute walk.

It was still only 7.30am, and it was another night spent travelling. Once settled in Lem's house, we decided to rest for a while, as soon the metro rush hour would be starting. In the meantime Vera made us Chie and we had a light breakfast. When making all these travel arrangements, I was unable to book the compulsory bunks for the return trip. Today we had to go to the station and make the arrangements. It was there that we suffered one of our big disappointments. Such is life in Russia that things change overnight, as now we were told that the said bunks would cost $96. We didn't have any choice about paying if we wanted to get home, but it was more of a case of: *did we have the money?* To sort this out we had to detach ourselves from the already enormous queue, and after a lot of searching and sharing we found that we had enough for everyone to have the necessary bunks.

God was at work again.

Back into the queue I went, eventually getting to the counter, only to be told that there were only five bunks left (and there was seven of us). There and then I felt that we must grab what we could, so we took and paid for the five bunks. Then, somewhat despondently, we set off back to Lem and Vera's. Some decisions had to be made! Faced with such a situation, I went somewhere quiet. I preferred to be left alone to think and pray things through without interference. After assessing each member of the team, I believed that the two who would be best left behind would be Peter and myself. I felt that we two together could cope with whatever came our way. I also felt happier knowing that all the other members of the team would be safely on their way home. That decision made and accepted gave me peace of mind.

It was while we were at Lem's that Jean had decided not to travel back with us, hence the need for only seven bunks. In the past Jean had travelled to China with the Open Door ministries, and had friends there, so as we were already half way there Jean thought that she would like to continue her travels and pay them a visit. We'd had a very busy three hours but it was still only mid-morning, so as we were in Moscow, we just *had* to do some sightseeing. Naturally the Red Square, Lenin's tomb, St Basils and the Kremlin buildings were not to be missed. All of this meant a lot of walking and another ride on the Metro, and it was still hot, hot, hot!

Although this was an exciting time, there was an emotional price to pay. This country had been through a very, very hard time over the previous seventy years of communist rule, and we were surrounded by the evidence of that time. From the pavement to the Metro platform there were maybe 75 to 100 steps, and on each side of each step stood a shabbily dressed person, each holding something, something to sell: things like a book, a table, a chair, a puppy, a standard lamp, a bunch of flowers, a bunch of onions, an article of clothing, an ornament. These people were the poorest of the poor, and they stood there all day and probably every day. We had one very young girl approach us. I estimated her to be no more than 16 years old. She held a tightly wrapped bundle in her arms and was crying, "Feed my baby, feed my baby." Tanya said that we must not help these people in any way. With a Christian heart ticking away I personally found that very hard, but it was wise instruction, as everything about us screamed out that we were westerners. Once we would put our hands in our pockets, we would be descended upon by countless people and the situation could get dangerous, so we passed them by.

Making our way to Red Square meant walking through the streets, which I found very interesting. I liked looking at the various types of architecture, the transport, trams, buses, and lorries, the women working on building sites, ready with a nice smile for the camera. Red Square: this was where the communist leaders held their Easter parades, showing off their military might. The guards were parading up and down in front of Lenin's tomb.

We saw one part of a vast array of buildings – they evidently liked their golden tops, as most of the buildings were topped with gold or red stars. All the buildings and grounds were well set out and extremely well cared for. From the Kremlin we went to see St. Basils, which was situated at the far end of Red Square; 'red' in old Russian means 'beautiful', and I do consider this area to be beautiful. It is decorative, ornate, and colourful. It was the Tsar, Ivan the Terrible, who commissioned the building of St. Basils, and a story tells that, on its completion, he asked the architects and builders if they could reproduce the Basilica without the drawings at some later date. They all said, "Yes!" at which point Ivan had all their eyes pulled out, because he wanted St. Basils to be unique. Having read a little about this man, I can well believe the story. He was not a nice person and well deserved his soubriquet: 'The Terrible'.

It was time to go back to Lev and Vera's, where we needed to pick up the luggage and make tracks for the station. The train left at 8.10pm. Once there, we made one last effort to see if there was any chance for two more bunks, but no, so we said our *'cheerio's* and parted company. Jean, Peter and I headed back to Lev's flat to spend what we hoped would be just one more night.

Another day dawned, and it was an early start, as Jean needed to go to the Chinese embassy to get her Visa. I felt it wise to go with her. The first thing we needed was the direction to get there. We were on our own now, as Tanya had gone off to see her family. Finding the embassy was not too difficult, but once there we found that half of China was there too! The embassy consisted of just one small room, with one clerk serving everyone. The place was just a mass of bodies and, naturally, all speaking Chinese. I understood then why the good Lord had prompted me to accompany Jean: the good news was that the Chinese being a small race meant I could tuck Jean in my arms, draw myself up to my full six feet two inches and force our way forward.

We got to the two-foot-square window, where Jean said, "Beijing."

The man said, "Passaport Missee."

Jean handed over her passport. He then stuck four fingers up, and closed the window. Apparently business for the day was over. The whole business had taken about forty seconds. The four fingers meant that Jean should return in four days' time. Everyone trooped outside and departed. Once outside, I voiced my concern for Jean. I highlighted the fact that as of that night, with Peter and I leaving, she would be in Russia alone, with no passport to get out, no interpreter to do any translating for her, and as yet no visa. I asked her if she would be alright.

Jean just touched my arm and said, "Bryan its times like this that we trust in God." Point taken!

If asked to describe Jean Frazer, one would be tempted to say that she was a little grey haired lady. Not so; Jean Frazer was a giant! Her life was her witness. And considering her age, she was an inspiration to us all. We filled the rest of the day up by just relaxing and chatting to Lev. Lev liked his T.V. and his football. He was a big fan of Lev Yashin, Russia's goalkeeper. Come evening, and it was time for Peter and I to start making tracks for the station. Once there we needed to secure two bunks. Getting there early meant that we gave ourselves a good chance of success, and we were (successful, that is). Bunks secured, we were able to settle down for what we knew to be a long journey. Again the train left at 8.10 pm, which meant that we were 24 hours behind the other team members.

Relaxing on the train and stretching out on the bunks soon served to show just how tired we were, and for a while we slept like babies. For our refreshments we had cold drinks, crackers, cheese, a tin of fish, and fruit. We again spent a lot of time watching the countryside roll by. It was still hot and sunny but always enjoyable.

We got to Oostende on time, and then it was on to the ferry and across to Dover. There we met up with the team, all glad to be reunited, safe and well. With Phil Ferris behind the wheel, we set off for Penryn: a steady drive, no punctures and a safe arrival. We had travelled over six thousand miles; visited places that I had only read about; we had lived in a different age and culture; met, shared, learnt, encouraged, and been encouraged by some of God's beautiful people. It was challenging, enlightening, stimulating, frustrating, tiring, and rewarding. Would I do it again? Of course! Why? Because, it's God at work!

And He was not finished yet. I didn't know it at the time, but I still had a lot more travelling to do. The journey was far from over. If one's faith is not sacrificial, you have to question its value.

THINK HARD FOR A VALID REASON

NOT TO DO SOMETHING.

IF YOU CAN’T FIND ONE,

GET ON WITH IT.

H.O.P.E.

It wasn't until I had been home for a day or two that I realised just how tired we both were, both mentally and physically. It didn't take long for both Sylvia and I to 'nod' off once we sat down, so for several days we just took things easy, nothing too strenuous, and if we felt like a sleep, we slept. After about a week we felt that we were back to normal and fell back into our usual routine.

I suspected that the rest of the team felt the same; that, plus the fact that I thought that they had seen enough of me for a while, made me think that we all needed some time to collect our thoughts about any future work along similar lines. A week or so on and I decided to have a chat with the team about where we were to go from there. Sadly, they had decided that the mission to Tambov was to be a one-off experience and so the team disbanded. I was disappointed, because I truly thought that between us we could have carried on, made a significant impact in other people's lives, and been an encouragement to the members of Emmanuel. But obviously it was not meant to be, and so I found myself with a team of four: Peter, Sylvia, Jesus and myself.

It was too soon to start thinking of another trip on the scale of Tambov. Besides, no doors had been opened for me to go through, and I didn't want to find myself leading God. I wanted him to lead me. I again reminded myself that I had asked God many 'moons' ago to use me, and I believe He had, and would continue to do so. At that moment in time I didn't know what the future held for me, but I did know that there was something in store, and that I needed to be ready and willing for whenever that might be. Luke 12 v 48 tells us, "Much is expected from those to whom much is given, for their responsibility is greater."

As someone who feels truly blessed in so many ways, the desire in me to fulfil this scripture comes easily, and as much as I believe that attending Church is necessary, I equally believe that for me there is no substitute for what I consider practical Christianity. Eventually Peter and I got down to some serious praying. We both recognised the fact that having seen what we had seen, there was a great need out there, a need by people who were not in a position to help themselves.

We both agreed that we must keep on raising funds, because no matter what we did, it would need financing, and as there were now only the two of us, we must be realistic about our aims. After much prayerful thought we decided to have some fly-posters printed. We designed the cover, stating what we were all about, then spent our evenings tramping Penryn and Falmouth, popping the posters through people's letterboxes. Also we explained that we would be calling again in two weeks time to see what the response was. We headed the leaflet, H.O.P.E. Helping the Oppressed People of Europe.

I am happy to say that the response was very good and so, over a period of several weeks, we had to spend a lot of time collecting all the 'goods' given to us. It was mostly clothes, toys, and bric-a-brac. We got so much that we had to ask a local farmer for the use of his barn to store it all in. We found the bric-a-brac helpful. By selling it, it helped with our fund raising.
The next challenge was to get enough cardboard boxes to put it all in.

We also thought it best if all the boxes were the same size, which would make packing easier. So after a visit to the local industrial estate, another successful part of the enterprise fell into place. Having got all that we needed to start packing things up, we then started to separate the 'good' from the 'not so good'. Some people had just off-loaded a load of rubbish onto us. This we just got rid of. We felt that we only wanted to send quality goods to these needy people. They already had enough rubbish on their backs and we didn't want to contribute to that scenario, so, boxes packed and labelled, we were ready for delivery. Our thoughts now turned to transport: who would deliver, and where should we send it all? Having got involved in this kind of work, I found that there was a network out there, all manner of people doing all kinds of work. And so, after a few phone calls we found ourselves in touch with a man called Bob.

God was at work again!

Bob was a man with this kind of work in his heart. He had set himself up in business, transporting goods to Eastern Europe and was a vital link between people like Peter and myself and the intended recipient of such goods. Bob had called his services *Mercy Missions.* Peter and I were impressed and felt that we had made a good choice.

After a chat with Bob, and to fall in with his imminent travel arrangements, we decided that Bosnia with all its recently well-publicised troubles would be a good place to send these goods. Naturally there was a financial cost involved. Bob had his expenses to pay: fuel, insurance, ferry crossings, etc. Again our decision to keep on fund raising proved to be a wise one. So arrangements were made to meet up with Bob one Sunday morning at Carnon Downs's roundabout, guide him to the barn where all our precious goods were stored, and help him load up his truck. We actually had so much (180 boxes) that two vehicles were used. So, after systematically loading up, ensuring that what we considered to be a precious cargo was safe and secure to travel, a cheque was handed over and we waved goodbye to what we considered to be another satisfying and worthwhile enterprise.

At the beginning of this work Peter was attending Emmanuel church. Sadly he had now decided to leave Emmanuel and return to his previous fellowship. So, after our H.O.P.E. enterprise finished, he decided that, as he had other things to do, he felt it best to call it a day, thus reducing the team to just three: Sylvia, Jesus and myself. Sylvia was mostly in the background but always supportive. Without that support, this whole journey would have been much harder.

Having said that, however, Sylvia had branched out on her own somehow. Sometime before she had felt it right to get involved in the local Charity shop. The specific aim there was to raise funds for use in Eastern Europe, more specifically, the orphaned children of Romania, and although I didn't know it at the time, this was to prove to be another piece of the giant jigsaw. Meanwhile, I again reminded myself that I had specifically asked God to use *me.* Therefore the actual size of the team was of secondary importance. So, I impatiently waited for God to work!

At this time I found myself working on the Penryn by-pass, a new road being built by McAlpines. As usual, on projects of this size, before any construction started, destruction took place, and my job took me all over the site. I was constantly on the look-out for opportunity. It soon became clear that there were some buildings which had to be demolished, although there was not much wrong with them. It was just that they were in the way. So, after getting the necessary permission, I went on a little 'recce patrol' and found that all the inside walls were made of 'studwork' (in other words, 'timber-framing'), and that all the wood was still in first class condition. At this my mind kicked into overdrive. When demolition started all this would just be bulldozed away and dumped, and I believed that I could put it to much better use.

That night I sat down and put pen to paper and designed a set of bunk beds, flat pack style. After getting the necessary permission I then moved in, before the bulldozers, and stripped out from the building all that I could use to make four sets of bunk beds. That done I could now spend my evenings doing something that would hopefully be of benefit to others, and doing that 'something' gave me an inner feeling of satisfaction.

Once assembled and painted, I called on some of the children of Emmanuel to provide me with some cut outs of certain Disney characters: Donald Duck, Mickey and Minnie Mouse, Cinderella, etc, etc. These became part of the product and just added a little more interest and colour. I need to say a big 'thank you' here to Giles Jones. Giles came up with some much needed timber that enabled me to finish this work, without me spending some of the money that had been raised, a generous act on his part and one which was a big encouragement to me. I have long ceased to be surprised at people's response to what I call I practical Christianity. I suspect that having the time and given the right sort of encouragement, a lot more people would go this route.

Putting these beds together using dowels, nuts and bolts etc, meant that they were easily dismantled, bundled, labelled, and stacked ready for transport and as such would not take up too much space in a vehicle. *Where should one now send them to?* Again I tapped into the vast network of activity that was going on in Eastern Europe. I settled for Popesti, an orphanage in Romania. I must say that, although I didn't know it at the time, those beds for Romania turned out to be one of the first steps that I took, on what proved to be a long leg of this journey. The jigsaw was still falling into place. This journey that I felt that I was on was made up of so many components: things that had happened a long time ago, things that didn't mean much to me at the time but subsequently turned out to be an important part of this journey (one of those components being Sylvia getting involved in the local Charity shop).

I suppose that, as Christians, we all believe that everything we do is God's will but how can we be sure? I didn't know if what I did was truly God's will for me so I adopted a 'fail-safe' attitude. I would rather be guilty of doing something that was not of the Lord than be guilty of not doing something which was of the Lord. I satisfied myself that at least doing something is positive and someone, somewhere, benefitted. Not doing something is negative and no-one benefitted, and if one did what one did with the right heart then the good Lord would understand and His grace would come to my rescue, should I have need of it. In the meantime, I would just keep on praying and believing that…

God was at work in my life!

I believed that time is a precious gift, given to us by God. I believed that our time is limited, tomorrow not being promised to anyone. Therefore it is essential to use it constantly and wisely, before we lose it. When thinking of 'time', I am reminded of the little ditty that is chiselled into the granite work and built into the exterior wall of a church in Chester. It's titled 'Time':

When as a child, I laughed and wept,
Time Crept,
When as a youth, I dreamt and talked,
Time walked,
When I became a full-grown man,
Time ran,
When older still I daily grew,
Time flew
Soon I shall find I'm travelling on,
Time gone.

The problem with that little ditty is that it will probably be the older generation who will appreciate its significance. The older one gets, the quicker time goes and the more important time becomes, hence the need to use it constantly and wisely, preferably in service to others and ultimately to the glory of God. That done, personal satisfaction surely follows. Again, on the theme of time, consider the following:

A Paradox of Time

In this day and age;
We have taller buildings, but shorter tempers.
We have wider roads, narrower viewpoints.
We spend more, but have less.
We buy more, enjoy it less.
We have bigger houses, smaller families.
We have more conveniences, but less time.
We have more degrees, but less sense
We have more knowledge, but less judgment
We have more expertise, but fewer solutions.
We have more medicine, but less wellness.
We have multiplied our possessions, but reduced values.
We talk too much, but love less.
We can make a living, but not a life.
We can add years to life, but not life to years.
We have been to the moon and back,
but have trouble crossing the road to help a neighbour.
We have conquered outer space, but not inner space.
We clean up the air, but pollute the soul.
We can split the atom, but not our prejudices.
We have higher incomes, but lower morals.
We are long on quantity, but short on quality.
We strive for world peace, but have domestic warfare.
We have more leisure, but less fun.
We have more food, but less nutrition.
We have two incomes, but more divorce.
We have fancy houses, but broken homes.
And on, and on, and on.

Conclusion? **We have a lot in the window, but nothing in the warehouse.** So much for Time! I must move on; otherwise, I'll be guilty of wasting it....

I have to confess that patience is not one of my gifts. I always want to be active and doing something, so much so that in between these enterprises I needed to discipline myself. I sometimes found myself wanting to lead God, and I knew where that would lead. I was learning how to be patient and to remind myself that at the beginning of this journey, I had asked God to use me, not the other way round. As I look back, over the last few years and reflect on where I have been and what I have done, I can truly see how God's plan has unfolded, and all my prayers have been answered.

At the time of waiting, I was very curious as to where I was going next. I was soon to find out.

NOBODY MADE A

GREATER MISTAKE THAN

HE WHO DID NOTHING BECAUSE

HE COULD ONLY DO A LITTLE

VALEA CRISULUI

From the day that I started on this journey, all roads had led East: first Russia, then Bosnia, through Bob's 'mercy missions'. Then it was Romania with the bunk beds. In addition to that work, I got involved with Euro-aid, sending goods to Albania and Bulgaria, the latter being their initiative, with myself and others operating in a supportive role but all the time being led East. One of the things that I looked for in my God was consistency, so whenever anything happened, or something was said, or I got some literature, with eastern connections, I paid particular attention to it, asking myself, "Is this the good Lord speaking, and what is He saying?"

I sussed out a long time ago, that God is way ahead of me in all that I do, and, in the past He put things in place, which had an effect on my future. With Sylvia already firmly established in 'Faith, Hope and Charity', the shop in Penryn; and considering the fact that the sole aim of this shop was to raise funds for orphaned children in the East, specifically Romania; and although I didn't know it at the time; this was to be just one more giant step on this journey and one more piece of God's giant jigsaw.

Enter Frank and Barbara Morton: an elderly couple who lived in Longdowns. Frank and Barbara, along with two others, Graham and Barbara, from Penzance, were the trustees of 'Faith, Hope and Charity'. Some time before, they, like many others, saw the plight of the orphaned and abandoned children in Romania and decided to do something about it, and so 'Primavera Copillar' was born.

'Primavera Copillar' is Romanian for 'Springtime of the Children', and as a registered charity, these four set about raising funds to buy a dilapidated property in Romania, hence the shop in Penryn. Monies raised there financed the work in Romania.

As with most things in life, nothing is easy, and even with the best of intentions, these four good people entered into a world of chaotic bureaucracy they never knew existed, a legacy from the communist way of doing business. This coupled with the sheer logistics of doing a building job 1600 miles away meant that there was many a frustration lying in wait.

I had a great admiration for Frank. As well as his advancing years, he did not enjoy the best of health; therefore could not do any of the heavy building work. Other skills, such as electrics and plumbing, he could handle with ease, but the heavy side of things was too demanding for him. As there was a lot of heavy work to do, I guess that's where I came in. So between us I thought that we would make a good team: Frank's brains and my muscle!

As previously stated there were four trustees involved in Primavara Copillar and to my knowledge none of them were committed Christians. And yet, I considered what they were doing as Christian work and operating with Christian principles: the sacrificial giving of their time and money to a very worthy cause, benefitting others rather than themselves.

Frank and Barbara's home was also a small holding, which meant that they also had animals to look after; therefore they couldn't stay away from the place for too long. All these things put together meant that progress on the development of the home in Romania was very slow, and considering the need, time was of the essence.

Hearing of all this I invited Frank to come visit me, and we sat down and had a good chat about the whole situation. The end result was that I offered myself in service to the cause. The offer was accepted, and so I took the first step on another leg of this journey. Once again I felt that…

God was at work!

During the conversation that I had with Frank, one of the things to emerge was that they had not yet actually paid in full for the property out there. So, after some prayerful deliberation and a chat with Sylvia, it was decided to make, what was for us, a generous financial contribution to this cause, this coming from the money that we had raised for our mission work. With all the other work finished that I had been involved in (i.e. Tambov, the H.O.P.E. project, the beds, work with Euro-aid), I now found myself completely free and able to concentrate on this new challenge. I have to confess there was many a time that I had said to Sylvia, "I wonder who gets more out of all this, them or us, I feel so blessed and privileged."

Most of this work was time-consuming and extremely frustrating, but that frustration only served to intensify our prayer life and that alone made it all worthwhile. So, in 1995, we started planning what was to be my first venture into Romania.

Our destination, Valea Crisului, turned out to be a very small community, well off the beaten track and situated in the foothills of the Carpathian Mountains, northwest Romania. This was new territory for me; so initially I placed myself in Frank's hands, he having been out there before. The departure date was set, the ferry crossing booked, a work program discussed, tools and materials needed were decided on, documents acquired, and we were ready to go.

This was a 3,200 mile round trip, and we were travelling by car. For time and financial reasons we were sleeping in the car, so when packing up the vehicle we needed to be systematic and give ourselves space to spread out a little. It was essential that we got some sleep, because the road we were travelling on was one of the busiest across Europe, and we needed to keep as fresh as possible, hopefully to avoid any accidents. Also, when packing up, we needed to consider the weight factor, plus the fact that the car was going to be our home for the next two and a half days. We started our journey at 6.30 am, on a Friday morning, headed for Dover, crossed the channel, and landed at Calais mid-afternoon.

Now it was just a matter of putting as many miles as possible on the clock before dark. By evening we were well into southern Germany, and considering the time we actually got up that morning, we had already had a long day. The road that we were on was very busy. Even from the start, at Calais, we saw great juggernauts, marked 'Austria', 'Hungary' and 'Romania'. The good news was that at least we knew we were on the right road. The other good news was that on the continent of Europe these big lorries were not allowed to travel on Sundays, which made Sunday driving a lot more pleasant. Hence the reason we left on Friday.

We made good time and shared the driving, which enabled us both to have our catnaps and keep reasonably fresh. We also had one or two necessary comfort stops to stretch our legs etc, and enjoy a little snack, but always pressed on. We would 'bed' down about 10.00 to 10.30 pm, but sleep proved to be elusive with too much activity going on all around us. So, after much tossing and turning, we'd realise the futility of it and give up. And so, at about 2.00 to 2.30 am we would set off again. Driving by day was extremely hot, and there was a physical price to pay. Driving in the very early hours meant that the sun was not up. Therefore, it was a lot cooler and much more pleasant. Also the traffic was a lot lighter, so progress was better. Such was the pattern of our journey for the 48 hours that it took for us to complete it.

It was in the early hours of Sunday morning that we arrived, still dark, and no one around. With the whole village in darkness, no streetlights, the only illumination that we had came from the car headlights, and although that was better than nothing, the light was very limited. 48 hours and 1,600 miles cramped in a Maestro had left us both very tired, so we decided to just find a place to sleep and crash out.

It being June month, the dawn came early, and although we were both still tired, we were up with the birds. I had absolutely no idea what to expect of Romania or of the dwelling that was to be my home for the following few weeks, but the sight that greeted me was very depressing. Having spent forty years in the building trade, this had to be the most disorganised place that I had ever seen: debris everywhere, broken blocks, timber with nails sticking out, broken glass, no floors, trips and traps everywhere. The whole place felt damp, and in my opinion positively dangerous. I wandered around just to get a feel for the place, wondering, "What shall I do first?"

Considering our general well-being to be of some importance, common sense said we should get ourselves organised, so, after making safe passage to the car, we started to unload our belongings. That done, it was breakfast time. With no heat or water in the place, what we could or couldn't do was very limited. So breakfast was just a bowl of cereal and a piece of bread and jam.

As stated, it was a Sunday, and it was proving to be a fine day weather-wise: warm and sunny. As I was to learn, nothing much happened on the Sabbath out there. Frank, having been here before, was known by the locals; the word soon got around, "The Englishmen are here," and people started arriving. "A call from outside, Mister Frank," and a lady came in carrying a bowl of eggs. Later, "another call, Mister Frank," and someone else wandered in carrying a loaf of home-made bread. This was the pattern of events throughout the day and Frank explained that this was normal procedure. I was to learn that, despite the fact that these people have very little, they are generous people and are quite happy to share what they have with others. Throughout the day my mind got accustomed to the situation that I found myself in, and slowly a plan of campaign evolved. So, first thing in the morning, I needed to make the place safe, which meant a good tidy up.

After finding a home for all our clothing, tools, and the food that we had brought with us, I felt it necessary to get my bed in order. A regular good night's sleep would be essential. With what I was faced, Sylvia would have had a fit. The bed was a small metal affair, with a very thin mattress and some very damp blankets, all quite smelly. With the weather quite favourable, I hung the blankets outside. This helped a lot, but the room itself was very damp, so I seemed to be fighting a losing battle. Eventually I decided that it was best to sleep with my clothes on.

With an outside tap for our cold water supply, it was beneficial to keep the kettle on. That way we not only could have our 'cuppa' but also have a shave and clean our teeth. Hot and cold running water (indoors): oh, how we take it for granted! Another test of mind-over-matter was the toilet, if that's what one could call it: a wooden structure, resting on two logs, spanning a small stream and running past the rear of the property, a plank with a hole in it and no need to flush. Ours and many others' passed that way; enough said! All was new to me, and I soon realised that I had so much to learn.

It was the evening of my first day, and I had already somewhat readjusted my thinking. Getting used to a different culture was going to take some time. Valea Crisului was just a small cluster of dwellings; many built using mud bricks, baked by the local gypsies in a kiln situated in a local field. Each house situated on either side of a dirt road had its own considerable-sized plot, from which they grew all their own produce. It was at the bottom of a valley, surrounded by trees - truly beautiful! There were no fences but everyone knew and respected each other's boundaries. There were plum trees, apple trees, cherry trees, walnut trees and grape vines - everywhere. The whole family worked the fields, producing all the vegetables that they needed.

Vast acreage of silage was cut with scythes. That was the winter feed for their animals. This silage was then made into haystacks, built in such a way that a centre pole, a stout branch from a tree, held them together and suspended from the ground to let the air circulate. I heard a rhythmic slapping noise. Curious, I followed the sound, and I come to the river, where I saw the object of my curiosity, one of the local ladies doing her washing. The slapping noise was made by the slapping of wet clothing against a rock. I had only been here a short while, but I was finding this a fascinating experience, and although, as I've already explained, some things were going to take some getting used to, I was convinced that I was going to enjoy the whole experience.

God was at work! And I thanked Him!

Monday morning and after a fitful night's sleep I roused myself to see what the new dawn had in store. It was early, 6.15 am, and already the sun was shining and the temperature was rising. In my working life it's been my habit to program my day's work the day before. That way I don't have to start the day by thinking what I shall do but (first things first) breakfast!

It was not a question of: what should we have? It was more a question of: what had we got? Our gift of eggs came to mind, so it was two boiled eggs, a piece of bread and a 'cana chie' (cup of tea); that took all of twenty minutes! Then it was a case of getting stuck in and starting things moving. There was an enormous amount of work to do and our time there was limited, so 'system' was important.

As stated, Frank was the man for the electrics and plumbing, so he wandered off and got started, whilst I felt my priority was to make the place safe. I needed to make space, so I started stacking things. We are talking 'trees' here, ten, twelve, fourteen inches in diameter and about nine or ten feet long, and there were many of them. They were used for scaffolding, shuttering, firewood, barrow runs etc. etc. As the day wore on, it became hotter and hotter. This was heavy work, and I was sweating so much that liquid, as opposed to food, was proving to be the more important to me.

By one o'clock we felt we needed a break. The sun was high and the temperature was in the high 90's. It was time for lunch! Again, what did we have but a tin of pilchards, bread, and cana chie? Thirty minutes later and we were back at work; by mid-afternoon I had some sort of order in the yard. Next, I started to clear the newly-built rooms inside. There were no floors laid yet. All we had was the ground excavated. Standing in the passage, looking into the bedrooms, one was faced with a thirty-inch drop, (80cm). This void needed to be filled and then capped off with the new floor.

To work efficiently and make the best use of our time, things needed to be done in chronological order. Hot water on the site was essential, and so Frank concentrated on the installation of the new water heater in the bathroom; after that, he brought in the cold water supply and connected the two. That was going to be a tremendous blessing, to be able to wash and shave. Having hot water proved to be a luxury! We had electricity on the site, but it was only something that Frank had just fixed up; so considering all things, water, heating, sanitation, food, compromise, enterprise, and ingenuity were the order of the day.

Whilst the practical side of things went on, Frank had to deal with the local bureaucrats. An application for an electrical supply had to be submitted, money had to change hands, which meant a trip to the local bank to change some English money into the local currency, Lei (Lay). I was fast learning that nothing was easy there. The local bank was situated in a town called Alesd, about twenty miles away. The first five miles of this journey was on unmade, very rough, track. Three or four miles per hour was recommended for safety reasons, as we couldn't afford to have anything happen to the car.

Something else I learned was that Alesd was the nearest place one could get any building materials from. Any trip to Alesd had to be worthwhile, so forward planning proved to be essential and time saving. As we were in need of cement etc, and not wanting Frank to do any heavy lifting, it was thought best that we would both make the journey. Considering that it was now six days since we had left home, I thought it time that I rang Sylvia. Another experience soon awaited me.

The local telephone exchange was next to the bank, and having changed some money in readiness, I went inside to make the call. The room was bare, no chairs or desk, but had a lady operator sitting behind a glass panel at the far end of the room. In front of her was a switchboard, which had had its heyday forty years ago. The switchboard was a large box-type affair, with what seemed like dozens of plugs that were being pushed in and pulled out as and when necessary. It looked like a scene from an American movie made in the 40's. I approached the glass panel and, after stating the obvious (that I was English and indicating that I wanted to make a call to England), I was asked in Romanian: how long did I want? I indicated, using two fingers and pointing to my watch: two minutes. I gave the number that I wanted by writing it on a piece of paper. A charge was made out. I passed over the money and was told to go and stand by the two handsets that were hanging on the opposite wall. What happened was that this operator made a connection with the international exchange in the city of Oradia. This was done by pushing in the appropriate plug, then cranking a handle. They in turn connected to an international line to the U.K and they called Penryn. Apparently this could take five minutes or five hours, depending on so many factors, one being getting an international line to England. I stood by the handset, as instructed, and after about 10 minutes, one of the handsets rang. The woman shouted, "Englishman" and pointed to it. I picked the set up and Sylvia was on the other end: connection made! Sylvia and I were enjoying our chat together when a voice cut in and said, "Englishman finish." Apparently my time was up, and so the phone went dead. Even a phone call in Romania is an experience. But I still left the place with a smile on my face. I found it all quite amusing: money in the back pocket, phone call made, electricity people contacted, cement in the boot, and it was off back to Valea Crisului.

We had done all that was needed, but (because of what was involved in achieving it) I felt that it had all been very time consuming: the best part of a day was gone and nothing had actually been done on site. It was frustrating, but that's the way things are, and we didn't have many options. We got back on site by mid afternoon, which still left us time to get some work done.

The site was tidied up, everything made safe, and Frank made progress with the electrics and plumbing. Floors were backfilled and ready to accept the flooring. That meant a trip to the mill for the planks.

Having measured the floors in readiness and not wanting to buy too many, I asked the man operating the mill, "How wide are your planks?"

"How wide is your tree," he asked.

How stupid of me! I should have known it wouldn't be that easy! Apparently, first of all, one has to go to the local mayor and get permission to go into the forest and cut the necessary trees. You then get local transport to transport the trees to the mill, local transport being a horse and cart. Once there, they are sliced into planks, about one and a quarter inches thick. Then, still with the bark on, they are yours, to do whatever you will. I would never complain about 'Jewsons' again!

Even though I realised that compromise was the name of the game there, I believed that to actually use that timber, at that moment in time, would be detrimental to the job. The trees were hardly dead and the sap was still flowing. Because of the nature of things out there, I noticed that a lot of the locals had stacks of planked wood piled up in and around their property, obviously maturing and being made ready for future use. I now knew why they did this. I suggested to Frank that we approach one of the locals with the view to buying some matured timber from their stockpile.

Those locals were good-natured people and were fully aware of what we were trying to achieve in their community. They showed a willingness to cooperate with us at every opportunity, so with the necessary wood in our possession, we could start to think about putting down the floors. They had a certain way of doing things there, so a little chat with one of the locals was needed. This in turn led to some practical help, and things started to happen. Progress was being made!

Our general everyday life was not easy: limited diet, the heat, long hours and the frustrations. Frank, in particular, found it hard. Having a chest problem, he coughed a lot, and he had to take certain medication to maintain his health. He was a private man, so I didn't ask too much, but I did advise him to go indoors at times to relax and cool down for a while.

The evenings were especially nice there. We had usually finished our day's work by 6.30, and by the time we had cleaned ourselves up and got something to eat, it was about 8pm. From the kitchen, we looked out over the green fields and on up to the forest. The place was a riot of colour, with all sorts of wild flora. Looking out on this vista, there were no buildings to be seen, so without man's intervention I could enjoy the real beauty of God's creation. I was reminded that there were multi-coloured birds, to-ing and fro-ing; a woodpecker hammered away at a nearby tree! The temperature was dropping as the sun went down. It was a time for reflection and I felt peaceful and satisfied.

Sadly, not so Frank! Evening meal over, and he just sat there, head bowed.

I asked him, "Are you okay?"

He looked up and wearily said, "I just wonder what I am doing here."

We were putting a lot of hours in, and it did catch up with you, so Frank was simply feeling the strain a bit. I felt it right to remind him of all that we had achieved so far and that we were there to help some of life's unfortunates, children who weren't in a position to help themselves, and that in the end the three of us would overcome, whatever: the three being Frank, Bryan, and Jesus.

I had tried to find out where Frank stood on the issue of Christianity, but he immediately shied away. I had a strong feeling that somewhere along the way he'd been badly hurt by the Church and just would not be drawn. A great pity!

The weather there was proving to be extremely volatile: hot and sunny one minute, then out of nowhere came big, black clouds, peels of thunder and a very heavy downpour of rain. On some occasions this would only last for half an hour. Then it was over. Then out came the sun, and within half an hour everywhere was dry again. The problem was that with every cloudburst of rain, our outside cold water supply turned brown, which in turn meant that we couldn't drink for some time, and a continuous intake of water was absolutely essential.

We now kept a wary eye on the sky, and when it started to look ominous, we filled up all our containers. We had learnt that it took twelve to eighteen hours for things to get back to normal, but it was a regular occurrence. Another lesson learned!

Now that Frank had got the boiler up and running, one of our luxuries was to be able to have a bath. That done, and not wanting to waste the hot water, I tossed in my work clothes and gave them a good scrub. With the soaring temperature that we had during the day, they didn't take long to dry, and I did need a continuous supply of clean clothes; "Plus," I thought, "there's no need to be a smelly scruff!"

Washing done, I would retire to the front steps of the house with my cana chie and just sit and think. With no T.V, no radio, no papers or magazines, the evenings were a real quiet time and proved to be a real blessing.

Literally across the road from us, there was a family, 'the Bradi's: Filimon (the dad), Florica (the mum), Christi, (their son), and Crina (the daughter). Crina, a four year old, would often be outside, amusing herself or talking to mum, as mum tended their vegetable plot. But I sensed that the Englishmen were a curiosity to her, as slowly, day by day, she had crept a little closer to me. That evening, I was sat outside when her little head peeped around the corner of the fence. I smiled, and she smiled back. Then I beckoned to her, and she very tentatively came over. This was to be the start of a beautiful friendship!

This young lady couldn't speak one word of English and I couldn't speak any Romanian, but from that night on, we sat on those steps and spent many an hour talking to each other. Through Crina I got to know the rest of her family, and, several years later and as I sit here and write of my incredible journey, I'm delighted to say that Crina is almost fluent in English. Most of the credit must go to Sylvia who, over the subsequent years, gave Crina a lot of time and attention.

Education in Romania is very good, English actually being a part of the curriculum. I believe that the time Sylvia and I spent with Crina gave her a head-start over the others in her class. Christi also wanted to improve his English. Christi was about nine or ten years old. Obviously he'd already been at school for a few years, but he didn't get much chance to practise his English. So after work each day, I found myself teaching Christi the English language (our God does have a sense of humour). Soon my evenings were filled with reading, writing and learning some new card games. The care and attention that we gave to these two children soon started to bear 'good fruit'. Filimon, their father, only worked about three days a week, so on the other days he would come over and offer his services. This was a tremendous help; increasing the workforce by one third meant quite a lot, especially as it was me that he was helping and, in the process, he taught me some of their building practices. All this was of invaluable help to me, saving time and moving the job along that much quicker.

Filimon and I proved to be a good team as we ploughed through a lot of work together. He spoke no English, except for, "Meester Frank", "Meester Bryan" and "Seelvia," but the language situation in no way inhibited our progress or the work involved. This was a good family!

It was now Saturday - market day - and we needed to travel the four (plus) miles into Bratca to restock our diminishing larder. But before that we were going to visit the local orphanage. This was a day that I would carry with me to my grave. Nothing could have prepared one for the attack on one's senses upon entering such a place. Words fail me here, but I cannot leave this episode of my journey unwritten. I walked up the four or five steps leading into this orphanage. At the top of the steps there was a large set of double doors. These were open. I crossed the threshold and that's when the smell started. It was offensive, but was bearable. Five or six paces across this foyer and we passed through another set of doors, leading into a large hall. The smell increased. There was nobody about, so we (Frank and I) crossed the hall and entered into a long dimly lit passage. Now the smell increased dramatically. It was so bad that I had to force myself to go further. There were no lights in this area - just a small window at the end of the passage. This window had a fixed pane of glass, which meant that it couldn't be opened, and it hadn't been cleaned in years. On each side of this passage were doors leading into other rooms. Towards the far end we could hear something going on, so we walked that way. A door was open. It was dark inside, but there was someone in there. We entered. This was it, and I was in hell. I lasted all of five seconds before I just had to get out. The smell was unbearable. My eyes were watering. I was gagging. I wanted to be sick. I went back into the passage and headed for the window, thinking that if I could see fresh air, it would improve things. It didn't. I wanted to spit. I did spit; I felt it would help cleanse me. It didn't. I stood there. What could I do? It's to my eternal shame that I just wanted to leave, feeling that I didn't have to be here, but I also knew that I shouldn't leave, believing in my heart that this was the very reason that God had brought me there.

It was then that I prayed, asking God for the mental strength to go back into that room. God answered my prayer. I wiped the tears from my eyes, drew a deep breath and went back in. This was a room about twelve or forteen feet square, and high up on one wall was a fixed pane of dirty glass, about two feet by eighteen inches. Other than that, the only other light in the room came from a naked 40 watt bulb, hanging from the centre of the nine foot high ceiling. It was much later that I found out that Ceausescu had decreed that no building other than his own place of residence could have more than a 40 watt bulb. I stood there, letting my eyes get accustomed to this dismal world. Slowly I began to see things. Around the walls of the room, were end-to-end of what appeared to be cages.

Since my first entry into this room, until now, only about two or three minutes had passed, but it seemed an age; I thought I'd seen enough. There wasn't much happening. I turned to leave, but by now my eyes had got accustomed to this gloom, and before I reached the door, I caught a movement in one of the cages. I stopped and took a closer look. It was then that the full horror of this place gripped me. At the bottom of each cage was a small child, lying in all sorts of filth (hence the smell). Nothing on God's earth could have prepared one for this. To say that I was shocked would be an understatement. I was appalled; I wanted to cry out. I felt so wretched and helpless. I had travelled the world and seen many a sight but nothing to match what was in front of me now.

I went to one cage and looked at the body lying there. There was no movement. The eyes were open but they weren't seeing. The eyes were glazed over and lifeless and appeared to me to be fixed on the ceiling. I realised later that, as these children had laid there all their lives with no other distractions, all that they have ever had to focus on was the ceiling. Therefore, refocusing didn't come easily or naturally to them. For all intent and purpose, these children were dead. I learned that these children had never left these cages since their arrival, whenever that was, and as far as I was concerned, they had been reduced to inert pieces of meat.

I looked at this, pale, expressionless face, with its blank fixed stare. I felt totally helpless and useless. I reached into the cage and caught hold of the child's hand. Pathetically I told her that she was loved. I told her that Jesus loved her. It was all so inadequate, and common sense told me that my words might not mean anything to this child. I took cold comfort that such words in any language, including the Romanian language, would have very little effect, simply because 'love' was a word that they had probably never heard in their young lives. But I did take a degree of comfort from the scripture, 'How beautiful are the feet that bring good news', (in any language) Romans 10 v.15.

She felt my touch and heard my voice. The head moved. Something clicked in her brain. She did refocus her eyes and they started to come to life. It was as if someone had switched a light on in her head. As I live and breathe, I swear the faintest of smiles creased her face. To this day I tell people, I have raised the dead. One of my prayers is, "God help these children."

Visiting another room, in this place, only added to my feeling of wretchedness and anger. The same sized room but occupied by children who were considered to be mobile (about twenty of them), all in various states of undress, some with just a pair of ragged shorts on, some with just a vest on, boys and girls alike. None had any shoes or socks; some stood, others lay down, whilst others sat with their backs to the walls. All appeared disturbed! Some were banging their heads against the wall; others were wailing. The place 'stank to high heaven'. Many children were covered in their own filth. It was hard to determine the age of these children, because they were so under-nourished and under-developed. There were four and five year old children who had not yet learned how to walk, so when one talked of mobility, it meant a crawl or shuffle. There was a woman who stood by the door with a cane in her hand. Apparently it was her job to make sure that no child left the room. This I learned was the only way that the children could be controlled using the minimum staff. It's been said that we, as people, can get used to anything, and I suspect that that is true, but I didn't want to get used to this. Being unable to actually do anything to improve the situation, I suggested we would take our leave. I found this situation to be an offence to everything that is decent and humane: an offence to the ears, an offence to the eyes and an offence to God Himself. Before we could take our leave, there was one more shock to endure: learning that this room that we were in was just one of many more in that enormous building. And I was to learn later that this building was just one of many in the country.

There are an estimated 100,000 children in Romania suffering this way. It's an odd way of thinking, but the figure of 100,000 is encouraging because at one time the number of children suffering in this way was estimated to be 500,000, so the situation is getting better, albeit slowly.

It's very hard to comprehend a situation like this. Hygiene was virtually non-existent, and wanting to maintain a decree of hygiene whilst there, one of the things that Frank and I did was to put all our rubbish into plastic bags. When we went to Alesd, we threw it all into the town skip. Arriving in our machine, we were soon noticed, and within thirty seconds of throwing our rubbish in the skip, maybe five, six or seven children scrambled amongst the rubbish to see what they could salvage. This is a way of life for them and normal procedure.

I felt that I needed to know more about this situation: how and why had come about? Who was responsible? Some research was needed. At one time Romania was a land rich in minerals, oil, coal, and forestry, plus an agricultural industry second to none, and was actually one of the commercial crossroads in Europe. The decline started in 1944, with the Russian Communists infiltrating the country, culminating with the complete take over by the Romanian Communist Party in 1947. One, Nicolae Ceausescu, was a member of that party. He, being an ambitious man, worked his way through the ranks until he became President in 1970. Romania has a land area of approximately 237,500 square kilometres, with a population of 22,000,000 people. By contrast, the United Kingdom has a landmass of 244,000 square kilometres (almost the same) and a population of 58,000,000. Ceausescu's conclusion was that they needed to increase the population, as the country was underdeveloped.

To achieve this population growth, he decreed that every woman of childbearing age must have four children minimum. To encourage the people to reach this target, no family would receive any financial help from the State, until the fourth child was born. And there would be harsh punishment for those who didn't comply. And so the seeds for this catastrophe were sown.

Naturally there is more to it than that. Ceausescu wanted to create a super race (à la Hitler). Another contributing factor was the state abuse of the land and the agricultural system. Ceausescu introduced a collectivisation policy (à la Stalin), and we all know where those attitudes led to: the result of this food policy was a massive loss in production.

So with very low income, the average family income being £10 to £15 per month, families got bigger with less food. Hunger became a way of life; so much so, that people started to abandon their children, not because they didn't love them but because they couldn't feed them. Many parents made this painful sacrifice for their children, resulting in the explosion of orphans and, in this case, the abandonment of children. In each case the state had to pick up these children and be responsible for them; hence the orphanage culture was born - created by man.

For not obeying the dictates of Ceausescu one of the punishments was for the man of the house to be sent away from his home and loved ones, usually far away and for a long period of time. Such a man was Theodor. Theodor and his wife, Maria, refused to tow the party line and paid a price for it.

Theodore was sent to Moldova, a small satellite state sandwiched between Romania and the Ukraine, in the far Northeast corner of Romania. He was sentenced to work in the mines for four years. Why? Because Maria only had two children and refused to have more. These people lived about four doors away from us and were good hard-working people who lived by Christian standards. Four years was a long time to be away from your family; not only that - it left Maria alone to fend for herself and two daughters. What would go through Theodore's mind during all this time? God alone knows. This was the kind of crazy ideology that led to this deplorable state of affairs with the children of Romania. To finish this sad tale on an encouraging note, as I sit here and write this, the Romanian government have applied for membership of the E.U. Before being accepted they have been ordered to deal with the situation concerning the children. And I know from personal experience that encouraging things are happening in that area.

We started this day heading for the market. So, with the horrors of the orphanage still fresh in my mind and the market place on the other side of town, we set off walking. Market day must be the weekly highlight, as the world and his wife seem to be about. Just walking through the town is an eye opening experience and one that I appreciated right now. It was helping to fill my mind with new thoughts and erase some of the recent images that I had acquired. Here was a mass movement of people and transport with many women walking to and from the market, each with a pig around their neck, its legs tied together in front to keep it still and to stop it from falling. Some were going to market to sell, others were leaving, having bought. There was a large gypsy population there, and it's my opinion that they were very clever people. Their livelihood depended on the things that they made: besoms, rakes, gutters, hats, leatherwork, baskets, and so on.

Transport was made up of horse and cart, cow and cart, water buffalo and cart. Some of the carts had wooden wheels, some rubber. There were flocks of geese, plus sheep, goats, and ponies, horses with foals, all either being bought, sold, or bartered.

Many stalls had home-made produce for sale: lots of cheeses and yoghurts, made from goat's milk, or buffalo milk, many vegetable stalls, bric-a-brac, and so on. All livestock business was conducted by the river, which flowed by the market place. The reason for this became obvious when I saw someone buy a leg of lamb. They took the lamb into the river, and killed it. The river took care of the blood flow. Then they cut off a leg, stuffed it into a bag and off they went. Hey presto; you asked for a leg of lamb and you got a leg of lamb!

Naturally, with a hot day like that one, the flies were out in force, and hygiene was unheard of. I suggested to Frank that we would only buy canned stuff or stuff that we could boil, like eggs, etc. That, with a loaf of bread, would do me. Once again I'd had enough of the local culture. I could only take it in small doses, so shopping done, we made tracks for home and what I considered to be more pleasant surroundings.

Mahila was a local lady and lived not too far away. She had a strong Christian faith and knew where I stood with the Lord. As it was Sunday that day, she invited me to attend church with her and her two children, Gabriella and André. I readily accepted. We arranged to meet outside the house at 9.30 am. Mahila turned up with her two children and we set off, walking along the dusty road leading out of the village. I wondered how far we would have to walk because I had previously travelled this road for several miles and had never seen a church. We came to the edge of the village and Mahila called me and pointed to a pair of farmyard gates. We went through the gates and entered a courtyard.

Mahila pointed to a barn-like building and, after tiptoeing through the cowpats, we entered the barn. It was about fifteen to twenty square feet. There was a man in the corner playing a small keyboard, and it was already almost full of people, all sitting shoulder to shoulder on planks of wood. There was a wooden cross leaning against the wall (memories of Murschansk in Russia came flooding back). When we went in, they all shuffled up and made way for the Englishman and his escort.

As usual it was very hot, so the doors were left open, and with the continual arrival of people, all travelling by foot, the congregation grew. Some were either standing outside or had improvised some form of seating, straw bales or upturned buckets etc. The service started. There were chickens and geese wandering about, both making their relevant noises, and there were cows outside doing their mooing. A local man conducted the service and a lay preacher brought the word. I was given a special welcome and made to feel quite at home. Naturally, I didn't understand a word that was said, but it didn't make any difference. I said my own prayers, and I hummed to the music. I was with God's people. I looked around. It couldn't have been more basic, and being in a barn seemed so significant, so different from the opulence of Emmanuel church. Mostly the congregation was made up of people of a mature age, which indicated to me that they had lived most of their lives through the communist years, years of oppression and deprivation. Yet they were still here, praising the Lord and giving thanks. I gave thanks to God for being a part of all this. I was finding it all an amazing experience. These people had been through the refining fire and had come through with fervour for God which took my understanding of the Christian faith to a higher level.

Service over, and I left with a big smile on my face; it was another first in my life: singing praises to the good Lord with cows, chickens and geese as a backing group. Wonderful! Another one for the archives!

Sunday evening, and we were invited to Mahila's for a meal and another strange custom. They served the guests. They didn't eat with them. I didn't feel too happy with this arrangement and suggested that we all ate together. All agreed and the result was a happy and joyful evening. Gabriella spoke very good English, so conversation was less of a problem. Gabriella told me that she learned her English watching Disney cartoons on their T.V. It was here that I met Liviu, Mahila's husband. Liviu was not in church because he was not a believer. Mahila had asked that I pray for him, a request that I was more than happy to comply with.

Liviu worked on the family farm. It was actually his dad's farm. His mum and dad lived in another part of the house. Tradition said that when the time was right, the farm would pass on to Liviu. The father figure ruled out there and Liviu's father was very much into the old way of doing things. Liviu, being of the newer generation and having the new won freedom, wanted to get away and find his own way in life. I sensed a degree of sadness about Liviu, but he was a good man; he worked hard and looked after his family well.

We purposely arrived early for the evening meal. I wanted to look around the farm and get to know more about the way of life there. I quickly concluded that they didn't have an abundance of anything there, but they did have enough of everything: enough chickens to supply all the eggs that that they needed and some to take to market to sell, a pig to provide a litter, which they raised (some they killed and preserved, others they sold), two or maybe three cows. Naturally, they provided milk, some of which was turned into butter, cheese, and yoghurt etc.

They grew sweetcorn, and this had a threefold purpose. All of the corn was used for food: some for the table, and some for animals.

The remaining husks were dried and stored, then used for winter fuel. It burned well and gave out a lot of heat. Nothing, absolutely nothing, was wasted or thrown away. They had their various fruit trees: apple, cherries, walnuts and plums. They grew grape vines, fruit bushes, such as gooseberries and strawberries etc. When the time was right, they picked, pickled, and preserved everything that they could. They had large food storage areas around the house. That was because the winters out there were very severe: 20, 25, even 30 below was not unusual. That coupled with four feet of snow meant that nothing much happened during the winter months. With very little movement possible, they needed to be geared up properly just to survive those harsh conditions

Mahila asked me, "How many cows do you have?" and was quite puzzled when I said, "None." There were no mechanical aids there. Everything was done by hand: planting and harvesting. I watched Mihila and Booni (Grandma) planting potatoes throughout the day and under the hot sun. They were bent over. Booni would make a hole in the ground with a stick. Mahila would scoop out a handful of cow dung from her bucket, drop it in the hole, then drop in a seed potato. Booni would then back-fill the hole and both would move on. This kind of work was not optional; it had to be done and these were the two people who had to do it. When winter arrived, out came the handlooms and a whole new industry started up - such was life on a Romanian farm. We made lots of friends there.

Another phenomenon there was the weather. It was always so volatile. One could be standing outside in hot sunshine, sweating with the heat, and within minutes the place would go dark, as an enormous black cloud appeared overhead. There would be a clap of thunder, a tremendous pouring of rain, and rattle of hailstones - hailstones as big as plums! I ventured out to pick one up and paid dearly for bravery with the bruises. I travelled the roads and saw fires started by the lightening strikes. When such a storm happened at night, the whole sky lit up, thanks to the dramatic forked lightening. I found it all very exciting.

Our weekend over and it was back to work, with a lot still to do. I had taken down a wall between the kitchen and passage. No big deal - I just used a saw and cut through the mud bricks, then pushed it over. The biggest problem was the dust. Doing this gave us a nice big kitchen-cum-dining area. After all the 'making good' was completed, a new kitchen floor was laid, then a new floor throughout the passage. A porch was erected around the kitchen door, leading to the outside. A new window in, and we were ready for decorating!

Because the place suffered from a damp problem, I decided to concrete a path right around the whole dwelling. This would help shed the rainwater away from the building. That meant a lot of cement was needed, plus a lot of ballast. For the ballast, we needed to talk to a man who lived at the end of the village. This man had a truck, but the ballast came from the riverbed, and conditions had to be right before loading could commence. If the river was in full flow because of a flash flood, then we had to wait for it to go down. Usually it was the gypsies who did the loading, so they needed to be contacted.

Anyway, the order was placed. A few days later, after a full day's work done, we went to bed. It was 11.30 at night, and suddenly there was a commotion outside. Up we got, and it's the ballast, but they wouldn't tip it until we put the money in their hands. Fortunately we had enough, so working by torchlight, we guided them in, and the load was tipped. We had our ballast, and one hour later we were back in bed. Such is life in Romania.

The cement was now on site and I was ready to go. Filimon had agreed to help and said that he could borrow a mixer. "Wonderful!" I thought. The next day it arrived. It was an electric mixer, but to get it going it had to be encouraged by giving the fly wheel a spin (by hand). This had to coincide with the throwing of a switch. Once going, everything was wobbly and loose and the drum had a mind of its own. I christened it 'the Monster' and learned to show it great respect. Despite all, it did the job, and Filimon and I spent three days laying over 200 feet of concrete path, plus the steps up to the front door. This effort proved to be well worthwhile, as it made a major difference, not only with regards to the damp, but also with being able to walk around the property on solid and clean ground.

Another time we were in bed and there was a banging on the front door. Bleary-eyed we look at the clock: midnight. Nevertheless we had to go and investigate. It was the electricity men who had come to connect us to the mains. We dared not send them away as it could be weeks or months before they returned, if at all. Two and a half hours later, we made our way back to bed, very tired, but very grateful now that we were properly wired up. I'd got to the point now where nothing surprised me.

Once again Sunday was upon us and instead of going to church, Mahila asked if we would like to go to another village where Mahila's married sister lived. We agreed, but to make the trip really worthwhile we suggested that we would pay a visit to a local orphanage and asked if we could take three of the children with us, thus giving them a day out also. Permission granted, we set off on a forty mile drive.

With Mahila being a Christian there was soon a sing-song taking place in the car. Again I didn't understand the words but I did know the tune. "What a friend we have in Jesus." So picture it: a hot day, car travelling along, windows down, four Romanians and one Englishman all singing their heads off in two languages. I'm thinking, it doesn't get much better than this. And Frank, who was driving, was a non-believer. I wondered what he was thinking?

We arrived at our destination about 11.30 am. The family that we had come to meet were still in church, which was just over the road from where we were parked outside their apartment. Curious, I wandered over to the church and went inside. I found a spare seat at the back and just watched proceedings.

This church looked almost new. It was made of timber, and looked distinctly different from all the surrounding property. Service over and I started to have a wander around; it was then that I saw the plaque on one of the walls. It told of how some people from Weston-Super-Mare had passed that way, made friends with the locals, saw their need, went home and raised the necessary funds to buy the building. It was well thought out because the building arrived in 'flat-pack' style and was erected on the site, which was prepared in readiness by the locals. This place was like a beacon, situated where it was, and was a tremendous example of sacrificial love shown by the people who took this initiative. To me this is Christianity at work and in a big way!

Cubby was Mahila's brother in law. He, his wife, (Mahila's sister) and their three children were all members of this fellowship. Service over, they all wandered over to meet up with Mahila and the rest of us. After being introduced, Cubby said, "I have nothing to offer you but Christian hospitality," and then invited us into his home. This home was one of Ceausescu's creations; it was a dark and dingy high-rise block of apartments, badly in need of some maintenance and a lick of paint. By our standards, this place would be condemned. The apartment was very small, with just the bare essentials: a table, chairs, a tiny place to cook and plumbing, and I won't talk about the sanitation.

Despite the primitive conditions these people lived in, this family had a great deal of pride; all were immaculately dressed. The three girls looked like they had been made ready to go to the ball: pretty coloured dresses, shiny shoes, ribbons in their hair. With Cubby unemployed and state aid being virtually non-existent, I felt that this family was an example of triumph over adversity. We weren't sat down very long before a tray of chie and homemade cakes arrived. Everybody relaxed and it was a good time for all.

Before I left home I had asked some of the children of Emmanuel to provide some love goodies for me to bring and share with the Romanian children. This they did and now I thought it would be a good idea if these Romanian children could write a letter of thanks for me to take back, thus encouraging our children. As usual the problem was the language, but in this case not just the spoken word, but also the written word.

Accompanying Cubby, from church, was a lady who sat and had tea with us. During the conversation she used an English expression, so I complimented her on her good English. She said that I shouldn't be so surprised as she was English, from the north of England, and was in Romania to teach students in the Bible School, in Oradia. The really good news was that she could speak, read and write in Romanian. I felt that this was a Heaven-sent opportunity, and it reminded me of this exact situation which happened when I needed help with the Russian part of my journey. So I asked her if she would organise my letter writing, from and to the children. A few words with Cubby resulted in pen and paper being produced, and the job was done - wonderful!!

Time was moving on and we had to have the children back in the orphanage at a certain time, but before we left I wanted us to have a time of prayer together.

I asked this lady, "How does one say 'Jesus' in Romanian?"

"Christos," she said.

I suggested that we all held hands to show togetherness and then I prayed. I finished the prayer by praying especially for this lady from England. Prayer over, I said "Amien!" (amen), and all the children chorused, "And hallelujah!" Great stuff - I love it!

Time to go, and everyone got up to leave. This lady was staying behind and I was the last to leave the room, but before I could cross the threshold she caught my arm and said, "You will never know how much I needed that specific prayer, and, at this moment in time." I believe that there was a tear in her eye as she spoke.

Driving back to the orphanage now, the thought occurred to me: isn't God wonderful? He brought two total strangers together, 1,600 miles from home. We met briefly in a stranger's house, she met my need and I met her need, then we parted, both happy and satisfied. There was no doubt in my mind, that…

God was at work!

Monday was here again, so it was back to the business of work and getting as much done as possible before our time was up. Throughout the day there had been a lot of coming and going to a house just over the road: ladies carrying baskets of (apparently) food, lots of men working, hammering and banging. Frank said that they were probably getting ready for a wedding. This went on for the best part of the week and, sure enough, come Saturday, there was a wedding. It was for a man from Valea Crisului but the bride came from a village some miles away.

Frank and I were busy working away, when there was a commotion outside and a knock on the door. Apparently, the wedding ceremony was to be conducted at the bride's village. The minister who was to perform the ceremony had turned up at the groom's village, and as the groom had already left, the minister was stranded, and time was short; hence the knock on the door. Would the Englishmen rescue the situation and drive the minister to the other village?

Naturally we said, "Yes," little knowing what we were letting ourselves in for. We travelled over what could only be described as a mountain track, very rough, strewn with rocks and ruts, and sometimes we seemed to be hanging over the edge. It was a very slow and hot journey, at times quite dangerous, and one that should never really be undertaken by car. I found myself doing a lot more praying in that country.

Eventually we got there, and not wanting to turn round and rush back, we decided to wait and see the wedding procession. We didn't have too long to wait before the sound of a trumpet could be heard. At first, a lone figure appeared, a man playing a trumpet, waving it about as he went 'walkies'. He seemed to be clearing the way in readiness for the happy couple who were following. They, in turn, were followed by what I presumed to be the respective families. They all paraded through the bride's village - a very colourful procession. Then, somehow, they all made their way to Valea Crisului and the reception.

When Frank and I arrived back, we were considered the 'saviours' of the day and were given no option about whether or not we wanted to attend the celebration. So as we had left what we were doing and made this trip in our work clothes, we went and got cleaned up, and put in an appearance.

Once again we entered into the farmyard situation, only now it became clear what all the hammering and banging had been about. This farmyard had been transformed into the wedding reception hall. The roof was made of a plastic and tarpaulin covering, all tied to various buildings or trees. Rows of wooden tables with white paper tablecloths, seating made from whatever was suitable. The décor was branches and ferns. In the centre of all this was an elevated table. This was where the bride and groom sat, flanked by the immediate in-laws. In one corner there was a place for the band, a fiddle, a violin and an accordion. Formalities over, one or two speeches were made and the celebration started. The place was packed. I was told that nobody was invited but everyone was expected to be there. Hence the contribution from all the villagers: the men doing the work, the women providing all the food. The music was lively and vibrant. They had their own traditional way of dancing: a kind of rhythmic shuffle. The couple faced each other with their hands placed on their partner's shoulders and everyone, from the children up to granny and granddad, on the dusty floor, moving to the rhythmic music. After a while the bride and groom left the room, and there seemed to be an exodus of people.

I asked, "Is it all over?"

"No."

What was happening was, the newlyweds went to another room and waited for all the guests to file past, each one making a financial contribution to the couple's new start in life. I personally found this to be an ideal way to conduct a wedding. This was a large celebration, made successful by the community being involved and resulting in very little cost to any one individual - "Very civilised!", I thought.

This was proving to be another long day for Frank and I, and we needed our beauty sleep, so we retired about midnight after another eventful and surprising day and my first Romanian wedding.

Time was moving on and our thoughts were turning to what needed to be done before we left for home. With the water now laid on, we needed to ensure that all the pipes were properly lagged and locks were on all windows and doors. Nearly every village and hamlet there had its gypsy population. In Romania you have the poor, the very poor, and then the gypsies. They always live at the very edge of town and the conditions and squalor they live in is unbelievable. Everyone shuns them and stealing is a way of life for them. So we had to make sure that we left the place very secure. Our friends did look out for us but it was unfair to hold them responsible.

Frank's health had held up well and we had made a great dent into the work that was needed to be done whilst there. I was getting all my washing up to date. That night we started packing our things away, and Frank checked the car over. We had put a lot of miles on the clock since we arrived. Jobs done, and it was dinnertime. During our time there we had tried to vary our diet. One night, we had pilchards and bread, another a tin of soup and bread, another, boiled eggs and a tin of pears, another, jam and bread, and another time, a tin of salmon, a slice of bread, followed by an apple, and so on. Neither Frank nor I were what one would call domesticated animals but I reckon we were both survivors.

"So, what shall we have tonight Frank?" I asked.

We search our depleted larder.

Frank said, "There are some cornflakes here."

I said, "Okay and I've found a packet of custard powder."

So on the penultimate day, of our time in the valley, our evening meal was cornflakes and custard.

The next day we set off for home; all our goodbye's had been said, a few tears shed, and it was off we went. An early start was essential; there was a long way to go - 1,600 miles. Although we had made the best of the conditions that we had been living in, we were both tired. I felt that I could sleep for a week.

Reflecting back on the whole experience, I believed that I had learned a great deal, not only about other people, but about myself as well. I had spent over a month in a very special part of God's creation. That part of Romania was very beautiful and the people were a delight, the culture a revelation. If it's daylight, then there's work to be done; clocks don't mean a thing. After school the children help with the making of haystacks. Survival out there was a family affair. I'd even been invited to go wild boar hunting (I declined).

We had been made most welcome and shown tremendous hospitality. It had been an opportunity and a challenge, which I had enjoyed immensely. My eyes had been opened and my heart had been broken. The good Lord had blessed me and mended me. It's in these situations that the Bible actually comes alive. No matter what one does for people in the material sense, our greatest gift was Love. To stand among the many children we had met, and feel a hand slide into yours, to feel a pair of arms wrap around your legs, to see their obvious sadness when we left - all this show of affection left me with mixed emotions and I had a burning desire to do more of this work. After initially offering myself to the good Lord in service, I felt sure that He had already got my future well planned.

Home at last, and, for the next week or ten days, it was just a time of resting and recuperating, catching up with all that had happened in Penryn in my absence, both domestically and in Emmanuel church.

Sylvia has coped very well, so there was no problem on the domestic front, and Emmanuel just kept on rolling along.

Nevertheless it was good to be back home with Sylvia and to be back in fellowship with my spiritual family. The church family in Emmanuel had shown a lot of interest in this mission work and had been most encouraging.

After being back for two or three weeks we had a meeting with the other trustees, Graham and Barbara from Penzance. They needed to be brought up to date with the progress made. That done, the ladies who ran the shop in Penryn needed to be informed. Everyone needed to be encouraged, as they all had played an important part in that enterprise. It was at the meeting that I was invited to become a trustee of Primavera Copiilar. I declined the offer as I thought that my first allegiance was to the good Lord and I wanted Him to be my leader on this journey. The shop was maintaining a steady flow of income, which was encouraging, as it enabled us to plan the next stage of the development with confidence, knowing that we wouldn't be frustrated by the lack of finance. With that in mind our thoughts turned to the coordination and planning of the next trip.

When working in Eastern Europe one had to take into consideration the weather. It could be extremely hot or extremely cold. Winter months mean temperatures of 25 below and with heavy snowfalls. Under such conditions everything comes to a standstill, travel and building work included. So, considering that the thaw usually comes around early to mid April, we planned our next trip for May month and made all the necessary arrangements accordingly.

The aim that year was to get the place ready for occupation and, with the inside almost finished, it was felt that we had to concentrate on the drainage system. That meant a septic tank and soak-away had to be installed. We knew that this was going to present us with a big challenge. Being in a valley we knew that the water table was high, probably as high as two feet from ground level. So how did we tackle this situation?

When it comes to septic tanks in this country, all you do is go and buy a klargester from a builder's merchant, hire a J.C.B. to dig the hole, and then drop it in and backfill. A klargester is a large onion-shaped dome, made of high strength fibreglass; a domestic one is about ten feet high and eight feet in diameter, quite a large unit, and something which is quite unheard of in our part of Romania.

We met (the trustees) on a Thursday evening to discuss the way forward. Because we thought that there was no way that we could buy a klargester out there and we didn't have a vehicle big enough to carry one, it was decided that the only other option was for me to build a septic tank using shuttering and concrete, a big job when one considers that the concrete all has to be made by hand. There were no ready-mix plants for many miles.

Meeting over, and we all went home. The next morning (Friday) we got a phone call from the Newcastle area and a total stranger asked if we were the people who went to Romania.

Answer: "Yes."

He told us that he was leaving for Romania early on Monday morning, sailing from Dover, and that he only had half a load. (This is the network out there at work). He asked if there was anything he could carry for us. Tongue in cheek, we mentioned the word klargester.

"No problem," he said.

His truck was a 40 toner. The problem was, he was now loading for the journey and needed Sunday to travel to Dover, so there was no way that he could get to Cornwall to pick up the goods. What to do? We took his mobile phone number and said that we would call him back.

It was late Friday now and after a few phone calls we were in touch with Jewsons in Dover. After explaining the whole situation to the manager, he told us not to worry.

"When in the Dover area, tell the lorry driver to contact the manager, then call in to the Dover depot. They will open up for him and help load the klargester on to his truck."

With regards to payment, they would make contact with Jewsons in Penryn, and we could settle up with them - wonderful! We called back the good Samaritan, told him of the arrangements, which he said suited him fine.

"By the way," he said, "whereabouts in Romania are you working?"

We told him.

"What the heck," he said. "That's not too far out of my way. I'll drop it off for you."

Because of our remote situation, and the size of his vehicle, he couldn't actually drop it on the site, but he got it very near, and left it in safe hands.

Imagine it! Thursday night, and we thought that we were faced with the impossible. Prayers were said and the following Wednesday the klargester was virtually on site. That in my opinion was a miracle, brought about because…

God was at work!

Once again, plans were all made, dates arranged, work program decided, and we were ready to return to Valea Crisului.
This time we had decided that we needed just a little bit more comfort and care, so both Sylvia and Frank's wife, Barbara, were making the journey with us.

The last year had been my first trip to Romania and I hadn't know what to expect. This time I knew what it entailed and suggested a slight change of program.

"Rather than drive to the ferry, get on board, sail across the channel, arrive in Calais about mid afternoon, do about six hours driving, then try and get some much-needed sleep, it would be far better," I suggested, "to drive to Dover, have a nights B&B, have a good night's sleep, catch a much earlier ferry, be in Calais early to mid morning, then have a full days driving before we got some sleep. That way, on the first day, we would be starting off much fresher, and do a lot more miles."

All agreed.

This time we had a mass of materials to take with us, lots of clothing for our friends, plus tools and food. We even had six bicycles tied onto the roof. All this meant that the van that Sylvia and I were travelling in was 'packed to the gunnels'. To make sure that I was not overloaded, I made a visit to the local weighbridge station with an empty vehicle, got weighed, then went and loaded up, then got weighed again. Having documented evidence that I was not overloaded is crucial. One of the tricks at the border is to make such an accusation, forcing one to offload some of the cargo before they will let you through. The cargo offloaded usually ends up in the hands of the border officials; this I presume is considered to be one of their perks.

We left on the Thursday and, as long as we got to Dover by early evening, we felt that there was no need to rush, timing our drive so as to get there about 6 pm, leaving us with a bit of leisure time. This proved to be good planning as everything turned out well. Consequently, by 10.30 pm on Friday the 17th of April we were well clear of Calais and heading for our destination. What we didn't bargain for was the horrendous weather. The heavens opened, and it was pouring down with heavy rain. With Frank and Barbara in their own car, and Sylvia and I in a large Renault van, and with limited visibility, progress was steady, but not fast.

There was quite a varied load that we had on board, and ideally we should have had a manifest to show the customs. We deliberately chose not to go this route, as we didn't want to appear a commercial venture, preferring the low key, touristy approach. Nevertheless, the nearer we got to the Hungarian/Romanian customs, the more I prayed.

So first day out, and after nine hours solid driving in what I consider the worst conditions possible, we decided enough was enough. Come the next civilised rest area, we would take a well-earned rest. So after finding what we thought would be a nice quiet spot, we settled down for some sleep. It was here that I had my first doubts.

My watch read 2.40am. It also told me that I was losing my struggle to get a good night's sleep. I looked across the cab to see my wife Sylvia also struggling with the same problem, with little wonder considering the position she was in, her backside resting on our 'Porta Potti', facing the cab roof, but with her head resting on the dashboard, her legs at a 90 degree angle up against the back of the cab. Not the most elegant posture, but the best that we could do under the circumstances. The non-stop rain that we had had to cope with, was still hammering down, now amplified by pounding away on the metal roof of our vehicle. Outside we were surrounded by twenty to thirty juggernauts, many with their engines running, supposedly to keep their refrigeration units going. The car park lights were on, and there was much coming and going, with the slamming of doors.

Once again I readjusted the pillow resting on the steering wheel, and tried to settle down, closing my eyes with the thought, "What are we doing here?" 'here' being Southern Germany en route to Romania. We had left our cosy little bungalow, and our king size bed in Penryn 48 hours earlier, and swapped it for this. For two people who share 130 years between us, the question had to be asked, "Are we mad?"

Anyway, after about six hours of cat napping, we all agreed to make a start. 4am was too early to think about breakfast, so we just readjusted ourselves and hit the road. After about three hours we decided to have breakfast. I kidded myself into believing that it was bacon, egg, sausage and mushrooms. Actually it was a bowl of rain-soaked cornflakes and a piece of Jill Parson's cake.

The bad weather persisted but we made good time and covered a lot of miles, eventually getting to the Austria/Hungarian border by mid-afternoon. My prayers were answered because we sailed through customs with no problems. Once through customs, it was a 300-mile journey across Hungary to the Romania border and their customs. It's at the Austria/Hungarian and the Hungarian/Romanian borders that one could have problems. However, thanks to good forward planning, all our papers were in order, and once we had satisfied the local Minister of Health that the food we were carrying was not contaminated and was for our personal use, and that the paint we had on board was of acceptable quality, we were allowed to pass merrily on our way.

It was while we were driving through Hungary that we came across two police cars blocking the road. We had no option but to stop. I told Sylvia to stay in the vehicle. It's compulsory both in Austria, and Hungary, to drive with lights on, even in daylight hours. Having got out of our vehicles both Frank and I insisted that our lights were on and a little test of wills followed. Our passports were demanded and after some talk between themselves one policeman held out his hand and asked for money. When making such a journey some careful planning is essential, and we had worked it out that if we filled up at the Austrian border, we could travel right across Hungary without the need to fill up again. Therefore we had no need to have Hungarian money with us. Thus, I stated: no money.

The one that had asked for money started flexing his muscle and got a bit agitated. I continued to argue our case, using some humble arrogance, getting to the point where I held out my hand and timidly demanded our passports to be returned. Thankfully, another policeman, and one who seemed to have some authority, spoke to his colleagues. Our passports were handed over, and we were allowed to pass on our way with no money changing hands. Once away, I pointed out to Sylvia that it was 11 am on Sunday morning, just about the time that the people in Emmanuel would be praying for our safety during the service. Again I felt that…

God was at work!

During the planning of this trip, we had arranged that we would arrive in the valley around midday. This would give us the daylight we would need to unload both vehicles and get settled in that much quicker. Frank and I had others to consider now, others who would not rough it like we did last year.

Ten minutes before our arrival, the rains stopped. It seemed that many parts of Europe had suffered the same rains that we had endured throughout our journey, including this place, which we were told had been severely flooded. Fortunately the river that ran behind our property was a good run off, and in no time the place was dry again. The people in Valea Crisului were no strangers to this kind of weather!

The word soon got around, "The Englishmen are here," and within an hour our first gift arrived: a plate of home-made cakes. So after a cake and a 'cana chie' we started to assemble the beds that we had brought with us. The way we were feeling, it wouldn't be long before we would need them! I met up with some old friends, introducing Sylvia as I went along.

The next day, Frank needed to go and exchange our English money into the local currency and so, whilst in Alesd, arranged to have the famous 'klargester' delivered. Having Sylvia and Barbara there was a big help. They took care of all the washing and cooking, which left Frank and I to just get on with the work.

As much as neither of us minded the work, we didn't fancy digging the twelve feet deep hole that was needed for the klargester, and as there was a great deal of poverty in the village, we thought it would be a great help to a local if we paid to have it dug. So entered Geeta, a sad man, beaten down by life, living in an absolute hovel with just three small rooms along with a wife and three children (I think). He also had his brother-in-law and his family living with him. Geeta liked his drink. One thing I learned was not be critical or judgemental of these people; their lives have been very hard with little or no reward. I suspected that drink eased the pain. Geeta was a pleasant man and the job he had undertaken was hard and laborious, but he turned up each morning and worked without complaining. We made sure that he was well-rewarded for his efforts, not only financially but also with food and clothes.

As suspected, we only dug down two feet when we hit water, so it was off to town to buy a pump. Now, as the hole went down, we had to sink a sump alongside. Into the sump we dropped the pump, pumped out the water, going beyond the pit depth, then dug out more of the pit. After a while the water was coming in so fast that we had to keep the pump going all the time. It finally took ten days to get to the required depth.

We then dropped in the klargester, connected it to the already laid drains, and back filled with concrete, all the time keeping the pump going, so as not to allow the water level to rise and float the klargester. That would have been a disaster. If the klargester had floated above the level of the pipes, we would have had to dig the whole thing out and start again. Before this whole process started Sylvia and I had spent time in prayer, and once again this proved a worthwhile practice - our prayers were answered. When the klargester arrived on site, the locals had seen nothing like it before.

"Mr Bryan, what's it for?" they asked.

I had difficulty in explaining but once in situ, they soon realised what it was all about. We had several lengths of pipe left over. These I gave to Filimon, with an explanation about runs and levels for sewage control.

"Bryan," he said, "I watch you; I understand."

So, off he went and improved his own drainage system. These people were amazed at our technology and equipment, and they were keen to learn. One of my hopes was that we could show them how to improve some of the basics in their lives, without infringing too much into their culture. There was simplicity about life in that valley, and it would have been a shame to spoil it. Some of our western ways I wouldn't wish on anyone!

With the klargester in place, back filled with concrete and connected to the drain, Filimon and I hand-dug about a hundred yards of trenching. This was to take the run-off water which drained from the tank into land drains, the land drains in this case being plastic pipes that Barbara and Sylvia had drilled holes in. This was to enable the water to drain away into the surrounding land. Now, with the first and only flush toilet system in the valley completed and working, we had much to celebrate, and a grand opening was planned.

Another major problem that we had with this property was damp - damp in the original part of the building. The extension was fine, as there we had used some of our western building practices, i.e. putting in a d.p.c. (damp proof course) during its construction. But the original part of the building, which represented about 50% of the total, particularly the floors in that area, were rotting, and we couldn't keep the walls decorated.

Giving this some thought between our last visit and this visit led me to make a trip to Travis Perkins (building merchants), in Penryn. It was there that I was able to buy a saw, with one tooth to the inch, and with a set on the teeth that would leave a cut of about 3/16th of an inch (5 mm.) Also the teeth were tungsten tipped, which meant that the saw would cut through most things. We also bought a thirty metre roll by fifteen inch wide d.p.c. In addition to those items, a hand-held pressure gun was bought and several small bags of neat cement. Now I could try to put my theory into practice.

From the window sill I measured down to floor level, inside the room. Then I transferred that measurement to the outside wall by adding four inches more to the outside measurement. That meant that I had a mark on the outside wall that was four inches below inside floor level. Using my level, I then pencilled a line around the damp part of the property. Then, on this line a hole was made in the wall, big enough to get the saw in. I now lay on my side and started sawing along the line and around the property. I could only go about 1 metre at a time, stop and insert a metre length of d.p.c. Then, using the pressure gun, I pumped in some neat cement between the top of the d.p.c. and the bottom of the brick above. The combination of neat cement and the hot temperature meant that it was only a matter of a minute or so before I could repeat the operation, making sure that the second piece of d.p.c. overlapped the first by three or four inches. It was hard going, sawing through twelve inches of wall, lying on my side. Persistence and determination was the name of the game and by mid afternoon, the following day, it was 'job done'.

Success or failure of this technique couldn't be measured straight away as the weather was dry then, but time has since proved that every penny that was spent on that operation was well worth it: the whole house continued to remain dry.

The four of us worked well together, each getting on with our own respective jobs; a woman's touch was added as Sylvia made and hung the curtains. The place began to feel like a home, as opposed to just a building site.

Sunday came and we went to visit an orphanage in a place called Baille Felix. This place was more like a complex than the usual orphanage (I'm glad to say). It was a collection of purpose-built wooded units, set in nice surroundings. Each unit was home to eighteen children and each unit had a father and mother figure, who were allocated 'x' amount of money to look after the children's general welfare.

The Swedish Baptist Association supported this whole complex and it was a credit to them. That place set the standard: well organised, well run, highly efficient, with happy, smiling children everywhere. I went a year later, and it was obvious that some of the children remembered me by the big smile of recognition I got.

Ghita and Radiana were a married couple who had a big heart for their country's orphaned children, and they were responsible for Unit No.6. Communication was never a problem. Children there were taught English as a second language, and once they knew that you were English, they wanted to engage in conversation There were just too many of them, all chattering at the same time, but it was a fun time for me!

When we arrived, Ghita was busy cleaning a wound on a little girl's knee - she'd fallen. I asked Ghita if I could help, and she said that the problem was that they had no dressings or plasters for that kind of situation. To buy plasters might seem a trivial thing to us, but to these people it meant something quite different. When I first came to Romania the exchange rate then was 12,000 Lei to the Pound. A year later it was 52,000 Lei to the Pound. Inflation spirals through the roof annually in Romania. Consequently, the spending power of money plummetted, and life continued as a struggle.

Sylvia and I believed that it was only right to give some financial support to Ghita and Radiana We had chosen a good day to visit, as there was a birthday to celebrate, and a party was planned. All the children sang, "Happy Birthday," naturally in Romanian, and then we sang it in English.

The story of Anna and Theo, two young children, is both sad and joyful. They were found living alone, literally living under a plastic sheet in a field. When Ghita and Radiana heard about them, they insisted that they be given a home in unit No 6. Even though they already had a full complement of children, they still found room to take care of this brother and sister, and they turned out to be a credit to Ghita and Radiana, studying well, with good grades at school, and progressing to better things. They are a living example of 'triumph over adversity'. Their start to life couldn't have been worse. Also, as they were older than the other children, they were able to help in looking after them. It proved difficult to find out the cause of this situation, and there was certain reluctance on their part to discuss it. I believe that some things are best left alone. Perhaps this was a part of their lives they wanted to forget, and who can blame them? Knowing and seeing them then, I came to the conclusion that it had been a blessing in disguise. Theo and Anna were two well-adjusted, courteous, smart children and both a credit to Ghita and Radiana.

Ghita and I walked and talked about things, discussing ways in which we could be of help to him and the children. Ghita took me behind the unit where there was a collection of bikes, all in need of attention and, as such, couldn't be used by the children. Again the lack of finance was the root cause, so we promised to go and get some parts to affect some repairs: inner tubes, brake blocks, puncture outfit and such. It was good to be able to help in some practical way, and as the money spent came from some of the generous church members of Emmanuel, I felt sure that they would approve of this decision.

What went on in that complex excited me. It also went to prove that a great difference could be made in children's lives when the church adopted a practical attitude to our faith. Mark 10 v 16 tells me that Jesus had a special place in His heart for children. He took the children in His arms, put His hands on them and blessed them. This then, was the act of someone who really cared.

The enterprise and initiative shown by those responsible there was tremendous. They had a large allotment, where they grew all that they could for the table, thus practising good stewardship of their finances. They had set up a little gift shop, which meant another source of income. All the mum and dad figures from each unit worked together, so although it was difficult for them, they were not going short of life's essentials.

If all of Romania's orphans lived like this, there would be a lot more happy children about. We spent a good part of the day there, and it was a joyful time, but we were a long way from home, so it was time to take our leave. I didn't think that we would have time to pay them a second visit, so it was 'cheerio' until the next time.

We got back to the valley late evening, but on the way back I saw something which quite moved me - a little girl, cuddling her doll. The doll was naked and headless - just a torso with limbs, but it was receiving some very special attention from its owner. I thought that such a doll would be swiftly consigned to the bin back home in England. These sights really made me stop and think. On arriving home we had a light meal, watched the sun go down, and went to bed - a good day!

With Frank, Barbara and Sylvia attending to most of the work inside, and with most of the heavy work almost done outside, I turned my attention to the dilapidated barn. As it was, the building was quite dangerous. The joists were actually tree trunks and stout branches, which had been there for many years and had seen better days, several being actually broken. I decided to 'bite the bullet' and strip the whole roof back and start from scratch. Having taken off the tiles, I found that they were a mixture of Romanian/Hungarian, with a few from Russia thrown in. (Is nothing easy out here?)

After stripping the roof back to the bare walls, I shuttered and made a reinforced concrete beam right around the barn. After levelling on the wall plates, I set off to the local mill to see what they had to offer by way of rafters. Timber acquired, I then started to straighten them, ready for use. I cut all the rafters, marking them left and right; all that done, I was ready to assemble. I was keenly watched by Filimon and one or two others, as this method was something new to them.

I also built in with this work a room, constructed in such a way that it accommodated two single beds, which could be used by visitors, should the occasion arise. If not, then it could be used for general storage. In less than a week it was job done, with everyone well pleased with the result.

Time rolled along, and the end of our time there was fast approaching, so we needed to start thinking about finalising each of the things that we were all involved in. We didn't want to leave some things half done.

Curtains were up, floor covering was down, kitchen units assembled and in position, plumbing and tiling finished, and everyone was feeling rather pleased. Whilst there, Frank and Barbara had met with the authorities with regard to the release of three children from the orphanage in Popesti (Tomi, Soani, and Maria). Over a period of time a special relationship had been established with these three children, so much so that these three had been promised a home there, but certain criteria had to be met before the authorities would sanction their release on a permanent basis.

Although meeting the criteria was frustrating and time consuming, it was realised that we were talking about the well-being of children. Since the plight of the Romanian orphans had been widely publicised, paedophiles had moved in, adding another problem for these unfortunate children to contend with. So caution was the name of the game, and this cautious attitude had my full support.

Knowing that things took a long time to happen out there, we just felt that it was time to get into the system, and as the property was not 100% finished yet, time was on our side. Hopefully all things would come together at the same time, the bureaucrats would be satisfied with our efforts, and finally the necessary approvals would be rubber-stamped.

In the meantime, Tomi, Soani and Maria had been spending time with us. They celebrated Easter later than us in England, so this was holiday time for them. The van was proving to be a magnet to Tomi and Soani. They kept cleaning it and then they wanted to sit in it. Soon the horn was honking, wipers going, radio on and lights flashing. Eventually I had to put a stop to it and insisted that they found something else to do. In Soani's case, that meant helping me!! Now I spent half my time looking for my hammer... and things were suddenly nailed down... my electric saw whizzed away... and my workbench was cut in half... bless him!!

These children had spent the whole of their lives in an institution, so this freedom that they were now enjoying was something new to them. They had probably never even been in a car before. At a particular meal that we were having, Tomi hunched over his plate and was gulping down his food in an almost animalistic fashion. Wanting to teach him some social graces, Sylvia spoke to him. He apologised but then explained that in the orphanage if they didn't get on with the eating process, the plate could be taken away for someone else's use, or the food itself would be stolen. We, Sylvia and I, were going through a learning process each day. These children were survivors and it had been a tough life for them.

Before leaving Cornwall, two or three of the members of Emmanuel church gave us a financial gift to use at our discretion. So let me tell you about Cornelia...

Cornelia was a lady who lived about six doors away. Barbara told me that she was among the poorest of the poor. I estimated that she was in her late thirties, early forties, married, but whose husband was mostly away from home looking for work and leaving Cornelia to look after the home and their two children, plus the family pig, and several chickens. This was a lady who would fill a plastic bottle with milk, then walk the four plus miles to Bratca and try to sell it, often unsuccessfully.

Here was a lady who had never had a new dress in her life, never had a new pair of shoes on her feet, yet never seemed to complain, and tried to keep herself smart in appearance. After some prayerful deliberation, Sylvia and I felt it right to give this lady an envelope. The contents of this envelope amounted to £70. The average family of four in Romania lived on less than £25 per month, so this, by their standards, was a considerable amount of money and probably more than Cornelia had ever had in her life before. This was made evident by her emotional reaction. She completely broke down, called her son from the house, told him what had happened, and both were beside themselves with joy.

We later found out that Cornelia had been abandoned by her father at birth. Her mother died when she was seven. She was then taken in by an aunt, who made it quite clear that she wasn't wanted; she got married at 19, and had lived in poverty ever since. I was told that the reason that she broke down was because that, for the first time in her life, she had been shown unconditional love, and it took two strangers from a foreign land to introduce it to her. Once again I believed that…

God was at work!

Many good things had happened in Romania since the revolution and one of them was the building of the Emmanuel Baptist Church in Oradia. This was the largest Baptist Church in Europe. The Americans financed it, and money was no object. Such a building was high on the list of demands that the people made once they had gained their freedom. The newly formed democratic government was quick to respond, making this one of the first major projects in that part of Romania, its massive building situated in a very prominent position.

They had five resident pastors, a music academy and a choir of about sixty or seventy, the men all with matching suits and the ladies with matching dresses. There are headsets in front of every seat; this facility enables one to hear the service in a variety of languages. They had five services each Sunday and a full house meant a congregation of many hundreds. There were T.V. monitors placed throughout the corridors and other areas, should the main hall be full. The place reeked of money: massive marble pillars, with ample gold inlay everywhere, chandeliers, marble stairways, statues, and fine art. There is no doubt that this was a magnificent building, but I couldn't help comparing it with the little church in the farmyard at Valea Crisului.

The difference between the two was not just in size. We entered this place as strangers and we left as strangers whereas, in the valley, I entered as a stranger and left having made friends, and feeling that I had been with family. The ambiance of this place did nothing for me, but in the valley I enjoyed the feel-good factor, and I had a smile on my face all the time. To me, small is beautiful. Having said that, however, the Emmanuel Baptist Church in Oradia wasn't just about Sunday worship. They had a good outreach program, a very, very large Bible school, which was used internationally. They also had a large acreage used for agricultural purposes. The produce was primarily for the staff and students in the school with any surplus taken to the local market and sold, thus providing a small income. This market garden was also good for providing jobs for many of the locals. I feel sure that what I have mentioned here is just the tip of the iceberg and there was a lot more going on than most people realised.

The principal pastor of this "church" was Dr. Paul Negru, an international speaker. He spent a lot of time travelling Europe and the last time that I heard him speak was in a small fellowship in Newquay, fronting for the S.G.A. (Slavic Gospel Association).

We promised ourselves that each Sunday we would have a day off, making it a day of relaxation, a change of pace, and a different environment, thus giving ourselves an opportunity to see something of the beautiful country. Towns, cities etc. left a lot to be desired due to years of neglect and lack of maintenance, but the countryside itself was a joy to behold. It, being a mountainous area, meant that there was many a beautiful sight to see: lakes, rivers, forests, all with an abundance of wildlife. There were still wolves and black bears roaming the high regions, and hunting was a favourite pastime for the privileged few. Winter months and skiing becomes big business in Romania!

As we travelled around, we passed through many a town and saw many an orphanage. All were awful, although some were better than others, but the people, in charge of the orphanages didn't seem to mind strangers popping in. As much as it pulled on my heartstrings I felt that I wanted to be there with them. We called in at one such place and were immediately surrounded by twenty to thirty children, all dressed up in their Sunday best. These particular children were in the care of Adriana, who was the daughter of Theodore and Maria, and they were the beneficiaries of much of the clothing that we took out. The children were some of the better-off children, who lived in this kind of environment. By Romanian standards they were reasonably well cared for and did enjoy an acceptable standard of life. And they did like having their picture taken! I went down the road about 50 yards and came back with a massive tray of 'inga tata' (ice cream). I don't know who enjoyed it more - them or me!

If ever I need to be reminded of the greatest gift, I just visualise the faces of these children and the way that they responded to human kindness. Doing that kind of work, I had come to the conclusion that time and money were the two things that frustrated me most. I would love to have spent more time with the children, and with the necessary funds could have transformed their lives. If only there weren't so many of them!

It's good to know that there is a lot of work going on in Romania and other countries by volunteers, trying to improve the living conditions for such children. These volunteers, being mostly retired people, do obviously have the time but they lack the money that is needed to alleviate the frustration that lives with the heart. I drew satisfaction from the fact that God knew what He was doing. My time spent in Romania wasn't just work, work, work. I had seen lots of nice things and met lots of nice people. Much had been overcome and I felt that our God had been glorified.

The building we had worked on was now almost ready for occupation. The authorities now had to be contacted and the place inspected; hopefully, it would be given a clean bill of health. As usual it took quite a bit of time getting the various departments together. But knowing this, we had our application in some time before. We were also blessed to have a young lady on our team who actually worked in the child welfare department. This was a big help as she was able to take care of a lot of the details.

Eventually it all came together, and an inspection date was agreed. Everyone who needed to be there was there, and to our relief and joy, all were mightily impressed; so much so that they made us an offer that we felt we couldn't refuse. The deal was: if we would hand over the property to the local authorities, they would take on board the financial responsibilities for the day-to-day running costs and staffing arrangements. Primavara Copiilar would retain ownership and be responsible for the maintenance. Also, they would pay all the running costs. They would have the right to increase the number of children living there. This thrilled us no end, as they actually doubled the number of children to be living there. This was a perfect ending for us. Three of the locals now had employment. New skills had been learnt, both by them and by us. Our circle of friends had been widened. We also paid for the further education of Cristi, Filimon's son. I felt that this was a good way of repaying Filimon for all the help that he had given us.

Twice, whilst there, there had been two serious accidents. The scythes they used were honed every five or ten minutes, which kept them very sharp. One man had an accident with his scythe and was losing a lot of blood. Frank felt obliged to get him to the hospital as quickly as possible. That meant a twenty mile drive, then a wait for treatment to take place and another journey to bring him home again. Another time a young boy was helping Granddad work. He was on the cart that was being hauled by a cow. Something spooked the cow and it took off, dragging the cart down a hill, and overturning it in the process. The boy was badly hurt. Again it meant another trip to the hospital, but it was good to be on hand to help in these situations. Showing a willingness to help made for good relationships, and many a time these country residents helped us.

As stated, the home that we had just completed was initially for the benefit of three or four children and a young man named "Soani" was one of them. Soani was not only an abandoned child; he was severely disabled. All down one side he was twisted, his spine out of alignment. He couldn't put his heel on the ground, couldn't raise his arm or use his hand, but was blessed with a brain as sharp as a pin and a smile as wide as a barn door. For all his disability, I was amazed by his dexterity and his joyful attitude to life.

We felt it right to go the extra mile with Soani and try to do something about his disability. That meant a trip to England was necessary, to see a doctor and have his condition assessed by a professional. As soon as we let it be known what was intended, we were put in touch with a man who specialised in the conditions that were affecting Soani. He not only agreed to see Soani; he offered his services for free. In addition, the Duchy Hospital in Truro was prepared to let us have the use of their facilities with a 50% discount. This was the kind of encouragement that I enjoyed, making me believe that we were operating within God's plan.

Soani Szilagy Alexandru, to give him his full title, was actually born in Hungary and was abandoned at a very early age. How he finished up living in a Romanian orphanage I don't know, but this situation complicated things no end. As an abandoned child he had no documentation - no birth certificate, for example. Without documentation, in Romania, one is virtually a non-person, so we first had to prove that he was a living person. Because his place of origin was Hungary, it meant many trips to Budapest, to trawl through a maze of paper work and being passed from one department to another. Because of the language situation, we had to have someone do all this for us. Budapest, being six hours away, meant overnight accommodation had to be considered, and there was a charge for everything that the bureaucrats did for us. This proved to be a costly business but well worthwhile.

The child welfare department became involved, as did the police. Everything had to be translated both ways, English to Romanian, and Romanian to English. Every page had to be paid for, but at least that way, all knew what was being said and done. Whilst all this was going on, fund raising was the big issue for us in Cornwall. In addition to the expenses in Romania, we had to get Soani and a 'carer' (he was not allowed to travel alone) from Popesti (the orphanage) to Budapest, from there to London Heathrow, and then on to Penryn. Assurances had to be given to the authorities in England that we would accept total responsibility for Soani at all times, and that at no time would he become a financial burden on the state.

Six months later and we had a birth certificate. Two months after that we got his passport, and two months later the necessary visa was issued. Paperwork completed, and thanks to Emmanuel, sufficient funding was on hand to enable us to make the flight booking. Now we had to tie up the dates between the doctor, the hospital and Soani's arrival. Soani's time in England was governed by his visa, so all this needed to be carefully planned.

For over a year I had been talking to the people of Emmanuel about Soani and what was going on. They seemed to have taken this situation to their hearts and were tremendously enthusiastic about it. People talked to me about Soani as though they already knew him. Again, I found this very encouraging!

Finally, Soani's smiling face appeared in our midst, excited by all that was happening to him, but a little apprehensive I suspect. He had a day or two to settle down before we met with the doctor, but the adrenalin was working and there was so much for him to see. He was very excited: first time out of Romania, first time on a plane, a long car ride. When I asked him what impressed him most, he said it was the houses, compared with where he lived. Every house looked like a palace - amazing!

Eventually the big day dawned. Soani and the doctor got together for the physical examination. Soani had cerebral palsy. The right side of his body was pretty useless. His heel was permanently off the ground and he just dragged the foot along. His hip was thrust forward, his spine was out of alignment, his upper arm projected at 45 degrees and he couldn't make a fist. All that sounded pretty grim, but having met Soani one tended not to sympathise too much. He was a resilient character, extremely mobile, and happy. I've actually played football with him. He was very intelligent and played a mean game of chess. I believed that Soani had a lot going for him and had a bright future.

Before the examination started, the doctor told us that he was going to ask Soani to get undressed and to lie on the bed, but we were not to help him in any way. He needed to see what Soani could do for himself. Instruction given and in about one minute Soani had stripped to his underpants and was lying down. The doctor examined him and after about twenty minutes told him to get dressed. The doctor then gave us his assessment. He started off by saying that if just half of his patients were as agile and mobile as Soani, he would be delighted. Considering the degree of cerebral palsy involved, Soani's mobility was amazing and he said that we should be extremely grateful. We found this encouraging. We were assured that the condition would not get worse, and after consulting with a colleague from the physio department, he gave us a set of exercises that would be of benefit to Soani. During all this time we had an interpreter with us, so that Soani knew exactly what was going on and what was being said.

Examinations over, we all made our way home. Soani spent a few days in Penzance with Graham and Barbara Hatton, the rest of his time in Penryn. He was introduced to the church members of Emmanuel, all of whom, I felt, took him to their hearts. We took him for walks around the coast; he loved the ocean, never having seen so much water before (shades of the Russians here). A free haircut in Falmouth was followed by a pasty, some new clothes and a new watch, all courtesy of brothers and sisters in Emmanuel.

Sadly the month Soani was with us passed all too quickly, and soon it was time to say 'cheerio'. I had known Soani for several years, and throughout all that time he insisted on never saying goodbye.

"See you again," he said.

Time and again these words proved to be prophetic. Soani was a Christian, he believed in Jesus, regularly said his prayers, and attended church each Sunday, so "See you again" would always apply.

From beginning to end, this whole Soani episode had taken about twelve months or more. Once again it had been frustrating, tiring, sometimes maddening, but as always, worthwhile and satisfying.

Soani himself has now moved on, happy and content with life. He is currently living in Oradia and is being taught skills that will eventually allow him to provide for himself. I believe that one day he will be just like everyone else, earning a living and making his way in life as a responsible adult. I have enjoyed being a part of his life.

With all that had been overcome, again I felt that…

God had been at work

and again, I thanked Him.

This proved to be the last step on this particular leg of my journey, but it was a journey, which was far from over.

TIMES CHANGE

TRUTH DOESN'T

CASA TORCH, DEZNA

As stated previously, God seemed to be one step ahead of me throughout this whole journey. As my work in Valea Crisului came to an end, so another opportunity opened up in another part of Romania.

"Torch Trust for the Blind" is an organisation based in Leicester. Their main function is to help people who are blind or who are just visually impaired. Not too long ago they became the beneficiary of a considerable legacy, with the stipulation that it be spent in Romania, helping the blind, orphaned and abandoned children out there. This help was to take the form of a specifically built home for such children.

Unbeknown to me, my name had been passed on to these people informing them of my availability and my willingness to be involved in this sort of work, resulting in an invitation coming my way. So, on my last visit to Valea Crisului, and before Sylvia and I set off for home, we drove the 160 kilometres to the town of Dezna, there to meet up with the local pastor, a man named Nicu Tole. The timing of our visit couldn't have been better, as at the same time that we arrived, one of the trustees from Torch was there with Nicu discussing a summer camp for Romanian children, a man named Mike Townsend, together with his wife Edith. The impending summer camp was the main topic of conversation between Nicu and Mike. At this stage, I was just an observer.

With the official meeting over, it was introductions all round; some light conversation took place, then it was down to business, the building of "Casa Torch", Dezna. Mike, being blind himself, had a great empathy with such children as these and as such was keen to get the project up and running. Leaving Mike and Edith to enjoy a cana chie, Nicu and I walked the two hundred or so yards to visit the site. I thought it would be wise to see what I was getting involved in before I made any commitment.

The site itself was just a heap of rubble, a partly demolished building. Having been exposed to the elements, and being made of mud bricks, the gable end just washed away. This was typical and commonplace out there, so the first thing to do would be to get the site cleaned up in readiness for the ground works to start. The finished product would be a three-story home for up to 64 children. This was a big project and would take a big commitment on my part, but before that became a reality, a lot of hard work had to take place.

Nicu was essentially a pastor and not a builder, but he assured me that he had a good general knowledge of building works and procedures; as the man heading up the Romanian side of Casa Torch, he and I would be working together. Nicu spoke reasonably good English. His wife, Adina, actually taught English in the local school, and his two daughters, Christina and Demaris, were also fluent in English, all of which meant that language would not be a problem.

Sylvia and I decided to spend the night in Dezna, giving me more time to chat with Nicu and get a feel for this project. One thing was plainly obvious: this was a big commitment - three, four, maybe five years. As I stood there at that moment in time, at a practical level there were only two people involved, Nicu and myself, and I was being asked to commute 3,200 miles to put up a building three storeys high, 100ft long and with a set of plans I couldn't read. I was thinking, "Surely this is impossible." I felt it was quite daunting but, as usual, also challenging and exciting. I practised my own philosophy and searched for an excuse not to be involved. I couldn't find one, so after some prayerful deliberation, I made the commitment and set off on another leg of this incredible journey. Again, I believed, that…

God was at work!

Back home, and as usual, Sylvia and I took time out to recover and rest ourselves. Although I had finished with the building side of things in Valea Crisului, we were still involved emotionally and liked to be kept up to date with the latest developments out there. Also Sylvia continued to help out in the shop; the shop was the source of all finance for the project in Valea Crisului. So our involvement with Casa Torch Dezna was 'in addition to', and not 'instead of'. We also had some lovely friends in the valley and found it impossible to just walk away from them. Nevertheless, Dezna was now uppermost in my thoughts, and I had to start thinking how I could start to make things happen.

The relationship between Nicu and I was still in its infancy, and we both had much to learn. Building that relationship by phone and letter proved to be somewhat frustrating and difficult, so much so that I believed it best to pay another visit to Dezna and spend more time with Nicu.

Visits to Romania had to be carefully planned, as they tended to have weather, rather than seasons, and the weather in winter meant temperatures of many degrees below freezing, meaning travel was virtually impossible. So, after communicating with Nicu with regards to the best time to travel, I found myself once more in his company the following spring.

We now got down to some serious planning. It was obvious from the start that all the work couldn't be done by just volunteers, and I had to consider the fact that Torch couldn't afford to pay to have all the work done by contractors. Time was also a big factor, and we both agreed that we had to aim for completion sooner rather than later.

After agreeing a strategy, we then started to visit two or three local contractors, getting prices for the ground works, exterior walls, roof etc, etc. This was where we had to depend on Nicu. He knew the language, the local currency and the cost of things. Nicu had the last word and we had to trust him and support him. Nicu was an honest man and quite trustworthy, and that was something of a rarity in Romania. Sadly, the more I worked out there, the more I had to live with that fact.

Setting things in motion was the main aim of that visit, and once achieved, I left for home, promising to return later in the summer. The strategy that had been agreed was: we were to get local contractors to put up the shell of the building, complete with roof and all exterior windows and doors, plus the inside and exterior rendering. In other words, get the place wind and water tight! Then I would move in and do all the setting out for partitions etc. Then, with the volunteers on board, construct all the bedrooms and bathrooms, studwork, plaster boarding, electrics, plumbing, and central heating, calling in local help if and when needed.

Until the shell of the building was up, there was not much that could be done by any volunteers. This was good news for me as it gave me time to go on a recruitment drive. It was not just a case of getting volunteers; it was a matter of getting the right volunteers and those equipped with the skills needed and be willing to commit themselves to such a project at the right time. In the first instance, I needed carpenters and electricians.

Running alongside this project, Torch also ran an annual summer camp for blind and visually impaired children, and to enable this camp to run smoothly, efficiently, and economically, volunteers were needed to help out in that area too. Considering the fact that the building was not yet ready for volunteer builders, and as I had promised to return in the summer, I thought, "Why not take volunteers to help out with the children's camp?" So, after my first recruitment drive I finished up with a team of youngsters from Emmanuel: Sharon Offord, Lois Richards and Hanna, a student from Bristol. In addition we had David from Folkstone, plus Sylvia and myself.

The timing of this visit was dictated by the dates of the summer camp, and those dates had to coincide with school holidays in Romania. Summer holidays, for these children, happened in the month of August, and August was the other side of the weather equation: very, very hot. During this particular visit we endured a high of 105 degrees. This was okay for the locals - they were used to it - but the team found it very hard, although it must be said that no one complained. After all, that was what we were there for, to sample the local culture, to see how the other half lived, to enjoy and endure their way of life.

We had all arrived there in Dezna travelling by mini-bus, using the well-used route across Europe. Once settled down, rooms sorted, introductions all round, everyone relaxed. The first job the girls had was to prepare the rooms for the arrival of the youngsters, then work out a program of events to keep them all occupied. I now had to drive to a place called Arad. This, about ninety miles away, was where some of the children would be arriving by train, having travelled from Moldova which was in the far Northeast corner of Romania and fifteen hours away. The train pulled in about 8.15 pm. It was easy to spot the children. Firstly, most of them were wearing thick glasses, and secondly, they were all holding hands, helping and guiding each other. Together with Georgette their helper, I guided them all to the bus and started the long journey back to Dezna. It being nigh on 10.30pm when we arrived meant that these children were pretty shattered, and although excitement was running high, all they wanted to do was sleep. By 11 o'clock they were all tucked up in bed and in the land of Nod.

The next day, I had to repeat the journey and collect another group. These children were from another area of Romania and their train arrived much earlier. Most of them were about seven or eight years old, and they knew where they were going, so once again all were excited. Travelling along in the bus they were all singing away (in Romanian of course). When they had finished they all insisted that the Englishman made a contribution, so I gave forth with my rendition of "You'll never walk alone", the Liverpool anthem, all to great cheers from everyone. After a few stops for 'Jimmy Riddle's and an 'Inga Tata' (ice cream) we got to Dezna by mid-afternoon.

For the first week of this camp we had about 25 children. Each of these children represented a tragedy of the human kind. Many of them had been abused, some were born blind, some went blind because of the lack of basic resources and some were made blind through ignorance. Alexander, for instance, went to hospital for minor surgery, and they accidentally cut his optic nerve, the result being blindness for life, and yet a funnier, happier character as one is ever likely to meet.

Many a time Alexander stood before us and sang, then told a story which had all that understood him falling about with laughter. I thought him a cross between Tom Jones and Jimmy Tarbuck. Alexander was about nine or ten years old. When the children arrived, all the clothing they had was what was on their backs. We could do something about that, thanks to the members of Emmanuel church. These were just some of the children who benefitted from all the clothing and financial help that had been offered and taken out on their behalf.

Since my May month visit some work on the site had taken place. Sadly, the standard was very poor (and Nicu agreed) so this particular contract was terminated. That meant that another round of negotiating was necessary with various contractors. This was a difficult time, especially for Nicu. One chap would only do the job if we paid him the full amount of the money involved: not only up front but put into a bank in Australia. I hoped that he was not holding his breath for it. Eventually we settled on a Christian man called Ghita, who headed up a firm called Tody and operated from Arad, but we had to accept the fact that he couldn't make a start until late summer. In the meantime the team was fully employed looking after the Romanian children, whilst I got on with laying a new drainage system in the annex, and building some much-needed retaining walls.

Sylvia insisted that I always finished work by about 6 pm. With the incessant heat I was always ready to stop by then anyway, and by the time I got cleaned up and had something to eat, the fun and games with the children were ready to start. The evening activity took the form of a sing-song with the kids. Sometimes a music group would come in and entertain us. Many of the local villagers went there for the evening. Lots of stories were told. Each one of the team gave a talk on what they did in life, and we in turn learnt about the lives of those young children.

It was during one of these evenings of fun that an elderly man stood up and started to speak. He was one of the villagers who had brought his grandchildren along to hear the music. It was usual during the evening for Nicu to give a ten or fifteen minute talk on the gospel. The whole ethos of the evening had got through to this man; so much so that he felt he had to speak up. He was crying as he said how glad he was that his grandchildren could at last hear the gospel from the Bible. He having been denied it during the communist years, as were many other villagers in attendance that night. I thought to myself, "What a powerful witness!" This was a spontaneous happening, and it was coming from the heart.

This is how my God works!

During the day, the children went off into the woods for long walks, sometimes going for a swim or just staying put and doing craftwork. Whatever they did was a first in their lives, some never having left the orphanage before. I found their enthusiasm infectious and there was a good feel about the place. This was also a first in the lives of Sharon, Lois, and Hanna, and not wanting to take things for granted, I thought it right to have a chat with them. Sharon said that on arrival she felt a bit anxious but had now settled down and felt more relaxed, having accepted the way things were. All three girls were looking forward to the days ahead and the challenge contained. Sadly, not so the chap we picked up at Dover. David was not suited for building work, even though he led me to believe otherwise. He had a bad attitude, and he spent most of his time sunbathing and reading, which was not much help to me nor the workload involved, but rather than fall out, I just ignored him and got on with things. Sylvia kept herself busy, washing and cooking for everyone and making sure that we all had a good intake of water. Her support and encouragement in this work was essential. She made the rest, and me, stop and insisted that I ate regularly - things that I tended to ignore if left to myself.

With no running water in our accommodation and no drainage system, we took it in turns to go to Nicu's place and have a shower. It was a very primitive affair. Wood had to be chopped, a fire lit in the bottom of the boiler, and a wait for an hour for the water to get hot. Then it was 'all stations go' for two people (separately of course). Then we waited for the water to get hot again and repeated the process until all had showers. But it was refreshing and it kept us all clean. I felt it right to insist that we start each day with a prayer. That would help us cope with whatever should come our way in that strange land, so full of surprises! One day we had some visitors: about twelve officials turned up. They represented the various local government departments: planning, sanitation, structures, legal department, the mayors' office, and so on. Such is the way of life in Romania that to get such a body of people together for a meeting was considered a miracle; not only that but they were delighted with the work that had been fdone, and everything got the necessary stamp of approval. Knowing what I know about procedures out there, it could only be that…

God was at work!

After the inspection was over, I was invited to the local café for a meal and a cold beer - all very nice. I was bombarded with questions about England and how we did things over there, and they especially wanted to know about the E.U. and the benefits of our association. All things considered, it had been a very good day.

Sunday was our day off but Nicu gave me a slot in his service each Sunday morning and the locals were encouraged by what was said. At the end of one service, and before anyone left, a lady stood up and was quite emotional. She explained that she was orthodox and had never been to any other kind of church in her life before, but that morning she said that God had spoken to her and said that she must go to the Baptist church that day. She went on to explain that she had never heard the gospel preached like that before and was amazed that people would come all the way from England to share Christian love with people in Dezna. She commanded everyone's attention for quite a while and made quite an impression, stating that she felt that she had been blessed by the Spirit that very morning. She also apologised to the team for the bad press that some of her countrymen had been responsible for in England with regards to the immigrant situation. This proved to be a very emotional and poignant end to the service. The Romanian sisters embraced this lady.

The Baptist Church in Dezna is a very small building, the seating equivalent to planed scaffold boards bolted to a welded metal frame. Many of the congregation were quite elderly and quite large, and this seating arrangement did not offer much comfort. Nicu explained to the people how he wanted to buy some cushioning material and cover the boards and back rest, believing that this would be of benefit to the members but did not have the £150 needed to make the purchase.

I personally felt challenged by this, so after some consultation with the team it was decided to give Nicu this amount. Some of the money came from members of Emmanuel church, the rest was made up from our own pockets - everyone agreed. Service over, a light lunch enjoyed, then it was off to Sertani, another Christian fellowship, to talk again about our Christian walk and what God was doing in our lives. This was quite a large church and it was packed: mostly young people, teenagers. That was good news. The bad news was that Nicu had neglected to tell us about this, and I was expected to take charge of proceedings with nothing prepared. My mind ran riot, eventually settling for each team member giving their testimony. This proved to be a wise decision, as the testimonies were wide and varied and as such captivated the audience.

The service over, we all trooped outside; there we were greeted with a nice cold coke and an opportunity to mingle with the many brothers and sisters who had come to meet us. It was 3.30 in the afternoon now, and the temperature was nudging a hundred degrees. Then it was back into the bus and an hour's drive back to Dezna. This was the pattern of our Sunday day off, travelling, witnessing, evangelising. It was tiring but again very encouraging as lots of people showed a much interest and wanted to know all about the strangers in their midst.

We were well into things now, so I thought I would just check with the girls again. Each said that they were enjoying the experience and apart from the heat there were no problems. Sharon then added that they had even got used to the toilet. My day was starting at 5.30 am. I tried to get some of the heavy work done before 7.30 when the sun broke over the hill and temperatures rose.

It was a red-letter day, as that day I put the finishing touches to the drains, turned on the water, tested for leaks and then ('Praise the Lord!') flushed toilets. Everyone was delighted. With the driveway levelled, retaining wall built, and some land drains laid, I could now relax a little.

I'd been virtually on my own doing all this work. David, the chap I picked up at Dover, had been AWOL since the previous Friday, and it was now Wednesday. He was about as much use as a 'chocolate kettle' (if you get my meaning?). He was off to Brasov on Friday, and I was glad to see the back of him. He wasn't missed.

With the pressure off, work-wise, I now spent a little more time with the children. Some of them could speak a some English, so it was good to just sit and talk with them. I learnt so much. Mihai was just such a person! He was one of the eldest of the group, at sixteen years, and spoke very good English. He was very courteous and considerate and told me that he wanted to go into communications when he left school. Being an orphan, and living in an orphanage, the lack of privacy made it hard for him to study, plus the lack of finance made it difficult for him to buy the things that he needed to move on.

Mihai told me that he got 40p pocket money per month and that was when the orphanage could afford to give it to him (which I suspect wasn't very often). Mihai was trying very hard to improve himself, so much so that I decided he deserved some support, which I gladly gave, again passing on some of the generosity as given to me by members of Emmanuel.

Time rolled on and soon it was time to think about getting ready to return home. But before that happened, the team had decided to pay a visit to the city of Oradia, on the Hungarian border and about sixty miles away. It was a pleasant drive, passing through some little villages, with lots of pleasant scenery. The idea was to buy some gifts for family and friends back home - memories of Romania. We never knew if we would pass that way again. Visas were not needed now for Romania, but one was only allowed to stay for thirty days. If you over ran that time you were in big trouble, and to get out of that trouble, lots of money had to change hands. To avoid this we had to make sure that we crossed that border in plenty of time. Once again new friendships had been formed and, as usual, part of me didn't want to leave.

Looking back over that month I felt that much had been achieved: essential building work had been completed, plans had been made, targets had been met, new targets set and a lot of happy children were on their way home having had the best time of their lives (their words). The team could feel quite proud of themselves.

Back home again and the team were all back safely in the bosom of their respective families with lots of stories to tell, no doubt. I am sure it was good for them. There aren't too many girls their age who have done what they did and been where they had. I now had to start a new recruitment drive, seeking men who would give up their time and come to help with the development of Casa Torch.

Since I started on this journey, I had made many contacts throughout the U.K., different people who were doing different things in Romania, all connected in some way or other with the orphaned children. So I started my recruitment drive by making a few phone calls. I also ran an 'ad' in the local paper, and in addition to this I used internet; soon the responses started to come in. Some people volunteered themselves, some put me in touch with others, and slowly but surely a list built up. Initially I selected the people who were more local than others. That way we could meet up, talk together, and I could assess them. David taught me a lesson on my last trip, and I didn't intend to make the same mistake again.

It was April month now, and my thoughts turned to another spring trip to Dezna. Through some dialogue with Nicu, a program was worked out for the team that would be arriving in August and to make sure that all the necessary materials would be on site in readiness for us. Before I could make too many arrangements, I needed to see that Ghita and his men had done all that would be needed for us to be able to carry on with our program. I find that programs and deadlines are great motivators and cut out a lot of time-wasting; time is a very important factor. The logistics of doing a job of this magnitude, 1,600 miles from home was daunting, to say the least, so I stressed to Nicu that when promises were made, they must be kept.

This proved to be a worthwhile trip as I could see for myself the progress that had been made, and I was encouraged. The walls were up and the roof was on, albeit minus the 'velux' roof lights. Still there was enough done to enable me to move in with some positive plans and make a start on the interior work.

Back home again, I started to sieve through the volunteer list. For various reasons, some were discarded and some had changed their minds. I eventually finished up with a small but very professional team. Neil was a young man (21 years old) and a fully qualified electrician. Rodney was fully conversant with all things to do with building and was a tremendous asset. Then there was Giles, the plumber, and central heating engineer, and Paul, who was just going to help out with whatever needed doing. In addition we had Alison, Rodney's wife, and their two children, Rachel aged 15 and Elliot aged 12, plus Barbara Monk and Sylvia. Whilst in Dezna, during the month of August, the orphans' summer camp would be taking place, and this is where Alison, Barbara, and the two children would be most useful - helping out with the entertainment and general welfare of the visiting children. Sylvia, as usual, looked after us, while Neil, Rodney, Giles, Paul and me got on with the building work.

None of them had ever been to Romania before, or embarked on such a journey, so travelling overland by bus from Penryn to

Dezna was to be a new and exciting experience for them. Not wanting the team to travel as strangers, I arranged a couple of social evenings together, a chance to relax, enjoy each other's company, and get to know each other a little. Naturally there were a lot of questions asked and answered. The workload was explained, responsibilities accepted, finances agreed, dates set, the ferry crossing booked, insurance taken out and a 'bed and breakfast' booked in Dover. Sylvia and Alison agreed to pay a visit to Asda to do some essential shopping, and then it was just a matter of watching the calendar.

Soon it was time for me to make a journey to Bristol, where I had arranged to meet up with Gordon Temple, and pick up the mini-bus. This arrangement was made, so I didn't have to do the eight hour drive to Hallaton, and Gordon didn't have to do the same journey in reverse to hand over the bus. Meeting halfway seemed fair to all concerned. Once home, and after three or four phone calls, people started to bring around all that was needed to make the trip successful: cloths, food, tools, materials, presents for the children, etc, etc. We had so much that we had to take out some of the seats to make room for it all, but we agreed that what we had was essential. We did fit it all in and managed to travel with a great deal of comfort, even managing to provide bed space, should anyone feel the need to sleep.

10am, Friday, 27th of July, and we all set off for Dover. I let Alison take the wheel for this leg of the journey, to give her some experience driving a well-laden vehicle and to keep myself fresh for the second leg on reaching Calais. The 'bed and breakfast' choice proved to be a wise one, as it was reasonably priced, nice and comfy, and with a full English breakfast in our tummies, we set off for the 7am ferry departure. Once on the continent, it was the usual practice: putting miles on the clock and getting there as quickly and as safely as possible. This we did, along with Elliot having the unique experience of having a roadside party in Southern Germany to celebrate his birthday.

We travelled across Europe on one of the busiest roads, but it was a good road, fast and safe, providing one drove carefully. Rod and I shared the driving, and I suggested, considering the cargo that we had on board, that 70 mph should be our maximum speed. It was a long journey, so approximately every four hours we enjoyed a comfort break, had a drink, maybe a snack, stretched our legs, and changed drivers. We started looking for a place to sleep at about 9pm, knowing that it would take a while. And so it proved, as we eventually found a nice place at 10 o'clock. It was a good choice, as it was clean and cosy with ensuite facilities. Because of all the precious stuff that we had on board, and not wanting to take any chances, I thought it best that someone actually slept in the bus that night. So since Neil was a young and single man, we all volunteered him for this responsibility. It must be said that he willingly accepted. This is where the provision of a bed space in the bus came in handy (good forward planning).

Up bright and early, after an absolutely fabulous breakfast and all for the cost of £50 per room, we found ourselves back on the road at 7.45am. We were soon well into Germany. Then into Austria, with its magnificent views of the snow-capped Alps. We followed the Danube for many a mile, crossed the border at Passau and travelled on into Hungary. This is where the big change happened: Austria, being quite affluent and Hungary, by comparison, being quite poor. After Hungary we went into Romania and again saw a marked change, Hungary being quite affluent by Romanian standards.

We eventually arrived in Dezna at 5.30am on the Monday morning, after driving for 36 hours. Everyone was very tired so we just went to bed. With all this being new to the team, it wasn't too long before faces started to appear and things started happening. The ladies got the accommodation sorted out, whilst the men checked out the building. With everything unpacked and a meal enjoyed, it left us with a bit of time to meet up with Nicu, Adina and their two daughters, Demaris and Christina.

Now, it was 'hubba hubba' time. The first thing we needed to do was to get on with the setting out of the interior rooms and start putting up the studwork, but to be able to do that we needed the 'lem' (wood). This highlighted the frustration of working in Romania with Romanians. Whilst over there, in the spring, I stressed that all the 'lem' must be on site for when we arrived. Promises were made, but obviously not kept. Nicu promised that it would be there some time that morning. It didn't arrive. Then it would be that afternoon. It didn't arrive. The same for Tuesday morning. Now niceness had to go out the window, and I started tub thumping.

Off I went with Nicu in his car; people were spoken to and eventually a load of timber was dumped on site. That was the good news. The bad news was that it was all two inches thick, just trees sliced up with the shape of the tree still apparent. Whilst one end of a plank could be about 16 inches wide, the other end could be about eight inches. Some even still had the bark on.

Now it was a matter of getting some local transport (a horse and cart). We reloaded the timber, and with me riding shotgun, we headed off through town to the local mill, there to have it all sliced into widths of four inches, thus finishing up with what was originally asked for: 4x2.

Wednesday morning, and timber was redelivered to the site. Any smiles soon vanished when I said that we needed another load of timber straight away.

"Why?" Nicu asked, also stating that what we had would last and that we were ready to start construction. We had considerable time - a week at least.

"Maybe it would," I said, "by Romanian standards, but Rodney and I would exhaust this pile by tomorrow morning."

Nicu found this hard to believe and left feeling that there was no urgency about my request. The next day, and we were almost at a standstill. Nicu saw this and now realised that he had a job on his hands if he wanted a continuity of work to take place. From then on he took more notice of what was asked for and spent many an hour every day running around the suppliers and keeping ahead of us with regard to the materials needed.

We had a site engineer on board, a lady named Viora. She was responsible for rubber-stamping the work that got done, and she checked on all the setting out, room sizes etc. Viora spoke no English, and as we did some things differently from the Romanians, I had to occasionally try to explain what was going on. This sometimes proved difficult and somewhat embarrassing for me, as I explained to her that we were doing things to an English standard, which was somewhat superior to the Romanian way. For instance, all the electrical work was being done using English materials, cables, power points, appropriate fuses, trip switches etc, etc.

This was a three story building, with stairwells at either end connected by a seventy feet passageway, yet no provision for fire doors had been made. I felt that these were absolutely essential and insisted that they be included in the construction. After some dialogue, explaining about smoke inhalation etc, all agreed. As they were not familiar with such doors, there was nowhere that we could buy them, so I had to actually make them and treat the whole door and frame with a fire retardant paint.

As time passed I developed a good working relationship with Viora, and she soon realised that we all knew what we were doing; so much so that her site visits dwindled down to maybe one or two per week.

When she turned up, I would let her wander around the building for a while, then approach her, draw my forefinger across my mouth as a smile and ask, "Is Viora happy?"

She would smile and say, "Bryan, Viora is happy."

Then off she'd go until the next time.

With the hours that were being put in and the concentrated effort of all concerned, Nicu was having a hard time keeping us going, and eventually we ran out of timber. But there was always something to do on the building site, so although we were sometimes not doing what we wanted to do, we did keep busy. Recognising the situation for what it was, I decided to measure up all the plasterboard that was needed and suggested to Nicu that we make a trip to Arad, buy it, and make arrangements to have it delivered. That way, when we ran out of timber we could get on with the plaster boarding. Also it enabled Neil to be able to cut in all his electric boxes and start the wiring. Nicu agreed.

Wanting to take full advantage of this trip, and as there was a supermarket type shop in Arad, I suggested to Sylvia and Alison that they would make out a list and do some much-needed shopping. All agreed, but before we could shop we needed to exchange our English money into the local currency, so it was a call to the bank. But this was Romania and nothing was easy. The bank had run out of money! So Nicu took us to another bank to get some. Before we embarked on the 180 km round trip we had to get some fuel, but the garage had no fuel; so again Nicu took us elsewhere. In all the time I spent in

Romania I learned never to let myself get too low on fuel. As soon as the gauge got below half way I sought to fill up.

With the plasterboard ordered, it was off to the supermarket, where the girls bought all that was needed food-wise. That trip took up a full day! We arrived back in Dezna about 6.30 in the evening with a nice meal waiting for us. Rodney and co. had been very busy in our absence, resulting in a lot of work being done. Rodney was the kind who didn't need watching. He had a lot of initiative. I wish I had six more like him. Neil, being the young man he was, enjoyed himself immensely. Unfortunately, with his workload and social life, he was not getting much sleep. He actually fell asleep at dinner one night. The nights were very hot there, so after dinner it was usually a cold beer, then into bed.

The girls ran out of eggs, and thereby hangs a tale. Rod and I decided to pay a visit to the local shop. Again, the language was a problem, this time being resolved by Rod bending his knees, flapping his elbows and clucking like a hen. When the staff stopped laughing, we got a dozen eggs and everyone went home happy.

Another day dawned, but things weren't too good. Both Sylvia and Rod were very poorly. With Rodney it was a combination of the heat and the midges. His body was covered with blotches and lumps. Both he and Sylvia were feeling pretty washed out. It was felt necessary for both of them to retire to their respective beds. Common sense prevailing, both agreed and actually spent the following 48 hours just resting. This was where Alison came in handy, being a nurse. Recovery was slow but sure, and the advice given in this case proved to be just right, because after that period of time both were back on their feet and functioning well.

Another day dawned, but this was a good day. It was Alison's birthday (prudence forbids me to mention the age), but party time was in the air. A cake was made, wine appeared and all enjoyed a barbecue. Alison was quite chuffed to celebrate a birthday in Romania, another first.

Running 'hand in glove' with all the building work had been the Summer Camp for the children. About ten days before, about 35 of them turned up, mostly blind children, but all with a sight problem. Nicu organised one or two evenings of entertainment for everyone.

One night there was an excellent group of singers/musicians and another time a full brass band. Other than that, looking after them was down to the initiative of all concerned. The children were be a real joy.

Emmanuella, about seven or eight years old, totally blind and left to herself, was one of the children who just rocked back and forth from the waist up and never spoke to anyone. On the evening that we had the group in to entertain us, Emmanuella actually spoke to one of the carers and motioned to the front. She was taken by the hand and propelled forward. She made it quite clear that she wanted to be placed in front of the keyboard. That done, she started to play and sing! Everyone was amazed. No one knew of this talent, as there had been no evidence of it before that night. Playing over, everyone applauded her. Emmanuella positively beamed (and I think that she grew six inches that night). Various activities took place with the children: a walk in the woods, a shuttle service using the mini-bus and taking all the children on the three mile trip to Minneasa, the next village, where there was a swimming bath.

On the penultimate night of the summer camp, the children were invited to say what the whole experience had been like for them. Every one of them said that it has been the best week of their lives and all wanted to come again the next year.

It was during one of my many conversations with Nicu that he expressed slight concern about the eventual running of "Casa Torch"; all this was something new to him. He went on to explain that when he was in school, many years ago, he had a special friend, and this friend went into children's welfare work. He longed to make contact with his long lost friend and pick his brains. Obviously there was nothing that I could do about that, but I did say to Nicu that I had a Romanian friend who was doing this kind of work in Baille Felix. This was the complex that was supported by the Swedish Baptist Church, with Ghita and Radiana managing hut No. 6.

I suggested that we pay them a visit and, once there, Nicu could have an in-depth conversation with this couple. This in turn could possibly alleviate some of Nicu's concerns. Nicu agreed, so off we went on the hundred-mile journey, Baille Felix being the other side of Oradia. After a three-hour drive we entered the compound, and after introductions, I left Nicu and Ghita in deep conversation whilst I made a fool of myself with the kids. After about forty minutes, there was a knock on the door and a man entered, wanting to speak with Ghita. Nicu's jaw nearly hit the ground. It was his long-lost school friend. This man was in charge of the next hut to Ghita's. This was the icing on the cake for Nicu. He was thrilled, and I have to ask myself whether this was another coincidence or could it be that...

God was at work!

Things moved along nicely; everyone got along well with each other. The children had a ball, and the work was progressing nicely. Paul and Giles were well on with the ground-floor plumbing and central heating. Neil was doing well with his electrics, and Rodney and I were ploughing through a lot of timber and plasterboard. However, experience had taught me never to get complacent about things, especially when they were going well. I needed to keep planning at least two or three days ahead, thus making sure to keep the momentum going.

The ongoing search for materials took me to many places: Sebis, Oradia, Arad and Timisoara. One time I told the girls that I was off to town the next day.

"Oh good," said Alison, "We need to do some shopping. We'll come with you."

Before we could shop, we had to go to the bank and exchange some money. Before we could get to the bank we needed some fuel. We went to the garage, but they had no fuel. Nicu took us to what I considered to be a back street garage, but they did have fuel, so we filled up. (This proved to be a costly mistake!) Next stop: the bank. Money changed, shopping secured, materials purchased, then back home - another eventful day!

Timisoara has a unique place in the history of Romania, as this is the place where, in 1989, the revolution took place. Timisoara Square is now virtually a shrine, and is well cared for, with modern shops, ornate buildings, and gardens. It's also kept as a reminder of things past: bullet holes in the walls and a plaque in memory of those who paid the ultimate price for their freedom. Again I wanted to know more about how and why all this happened; what triggered off the revolution that brought about a radical change in the Romanian life, and with it, the downfall of Communism?

Communism first took a hold of Romania in 1944, with its gradual insidious grip becoming total in 1947. 1947 was the year when Nicolae Ceausescu started to make his presence felt, working his way relentlessly through the ranks until he achieved his ambition in 1970 and became the dominant figure in the Romanian Communist Party. Shortly after that, he had himself elected into the presidency; from then on he ruled with complete autonomy, this coupled with a rod of iron. Slowly, and with the backing of the secret police and the military, he took a grip of all aspects of Romanian life, including the Church.

After a relentless campaign of persecution, intimidation, and murder, the church hierarchy capitulated and allowed the state to dictate all church policy and doctrine. Church attendance dropped away dramatically, finance dwindled, and buildings went into decay. These were dark days for the Christian church in Romania.

Lazlo Tokes was an idealistic young man when he went into the ministry. He believed in Biblical principles and had an innate desire to live his life accordingly. He took up the position of Assistant Pastor in the Hungarian Reformed Church in Timisaora, fully intending to preach and teach these principles to the congregation. At that time Leo Peuker was the principal pastor of this particular church and, sadly, he was a statesman through and through - weak in his faith and totally intimidated. Church life under Peuker had dwindled down to weddings and funeral ceremonies, as advocated by the state. This state of affairs suited the communists admirably, as the end result was a dead Church.

Things changed in 1987, when Leo Peuker had a heart attack, and Lazlo Tokes found himself promoted to a position whereby he could at last preach the gospel according to scripture. Wanting to right all the wrongs of the past, he took it upon himself to check back through the church records and to re-establish contact with former church members, those who had left when the intimidation had started. Slowly membership started to grow and the local community started showing a re-born hunger for the truth.

Timisoara is a university town, and with universities came students. It was when these young men and women started to swell the congregation to capacity that alarm bells started ringing in the local Communist headquarters.

Enter the heavy mob, and the persecution of Lazlo Tokes began. Apparently God had chosen well in selecting Lazlo. Here was a man of great faith, determination, tenacity, and commitment, a man who was not to be easily intimidated as subsequent events proved.

The intimidation began with armed police standing in front of the congregation at a Sunday service, thus *daring* people to come to church. Still they turned up. Next they took away Lazlo's ration book. Now he couldn't buy any food, which meant more hardship for his wife and child. The congregation responded by showing Christian love. They fed their minister and his family. Let's not forget that this was Communist Romania, and food was scarce!

Most people were hungry all the time. Sharing food under such living conditions meant sacrificial giving. Life became hard and unsafe for Lazlo and his family, so both he and his wife Edith thought it best to send their son Mat'e away to live with relatives for a while.

It proved to be a wise decision. Not long after, things heated up; Lazlo's home was broken into, he was severely beaten, and suffered a knife wound. A friend who had helped Lazlo was later found murdered.

Lazlo responded to all this by travelling far and wide, encouraging other ministers and congregations to join him in his fight for "Truth." It's estimated that at one service Lazlo preached to over 5,000 people. People were being encouraged, Bibles were being acquired and read, Church festivals were celebrated, baptisms took place, and the church came alive. Some eighteen months later the authorities realised that they had a serious problem and one that was not going to go away. Not wanting a martyr on their hands, they decided to exile the Tokes family. Notice was duly served and the date set: Friday the 15th of December, 1989. This meant him being taken to some faraway place, never to be heard of again. On Sunday, the 10th of December, Lazlo spoke to his congregation, knowing of the great personal sacrifice that the people had made on his behalf by continually supporting him. So, for their benefit and because of his trust in God, he decided to carry on with the crusade. He spoke to the people telling them of the latest developments and of his decision to resist. Lazlo just asked if some could be there on the Friday when the police arrived, as he wanted some witnesses for what was to take place.

Friday came and the police turned up driving a van, ready to load up Lazlo and his belongings. The van never got to be used. Surrounding the church was a mass of people, a human shield, all fully intent on protecting their pastor. News of this confrontation spread, and people sensed that something special was happening, as all day long more and more people kept arriving. It's been said that Timisoara Square, that day, was full of Adventists, Pentecostals, Orthodox, Baptists and Catholics, all standing together in support of this very brave man.

Ceaucescu had been kept fully informed of what was happening and set in motion the time-tested remedy: to send in the army and ruthlessly crush any and all opposition. Lazlo spoke to the crowd, urging non-violence, but as the two factions faced each other it became obvious that neither was in the mood to back down. All that day, all through the night, and into the Saturday, they faced each other. During that time the authorities made many promises. All were rejected. Late in the afternoon there was a movement in the mood of the people. Realising that they were shoulder to shoulder with many denominations and that ultimately they were all one in Christ, the cry went up for "Liberty and Freedom." This, coupled with the singing of a Romanian Patriotic song "Awake Romania" proved to be the spark that lit the touch paper.

Someone shouted, "Down with Ceaucescu."

Others shouted, "Down with communism."

The order went out: "Disperse or we fire."

The people had come prepared. They responded by lighting candles, and all stood there defiantly. The army fired. Many died; still they stood there. The army fired again, and still they stood there. It was now that the military saw the futility of their actions. Faced with the slaughter of literally hundreds of innocent people, their own countrymen, and with Timisoara Square running with blood, they laid down their arms and crossed over to the other side. Lazlo and the "Truth" had won.

A few days later and Nicolae Ceausescu, together with his wife Elena, were both charged with crimes against humanity, found guilty and summarily shot; Communism came to an end in Romania because…

God was at work.

Hanging on the outside wall of the Hungarian Reformed church in Timisoara are two wreathes. Alongside are four plaques, each proclaiming in a different language, "Here began the revolution that felled a dictator. Amen." I personally don't believe the Lazlo Tokes had any idea where his stand for truth would lead, but I do believe that he is a living example of what God can do with an ordinary human being, providing that that person is serious about his faith, someone who does not compromise his faith or offer a watered-down version. What does all this prove? Well to me it's a clear indication that times might change but truth doesn't. The gates of hell did not prevail.

Back on site and things were moving along quite well. Nicu was a 'happy bunny', and the site had been transformed. Our targets had been met, and the team was happy and healthy. Thoughts were now turning towards going home. Slowly we began to wind down. The girls got things together and slowly packed up the bus whilst the men kept going as long as possible. Eventually it was time for our goodbyes and we set off on our long journey home.

But all was not well. As we drove away from Dezna, I sensed the something was wrong with the bus, a distinct lack of power and down on speed - not much, but noticeable. It was making a bit of smoke. About an hour's drive to the Hungarian border, our speed was down to 55 to 60 mph max. Our bus was struggling! By the time we got to Budapest we couldn't get past 40, so common sense said it was time to do something. It was obvious that we were not going to make home. We pulled into a garage forecourt and phoned for help.

Help eventually arrived in the form of a local A.A. man. He in turn guided us to the local Renault garage. They performed a very brief examination and then declared that there was nothing that they could do. My personal opinion was, and still is, they just couldn't be bothered. I later found out that it was just the dirty (back street) fuel that we had bought in Romania and if they had just flushed out the system we would have been okay. I made contact with Gordon back in the U.K. He got in touch with the insurance company, and they in turn arranged a night's accommodation and flights home for everyone.

At the time this was quite an inconvenience as we had to leave quite a lot of our belongings on the bus due to the weight restrictions on the aircraft, but later all agreed that it was quite a blessing. The hotel we had was first class, and it was located right on the river Danube. After a sumptuous meal, we all went sight-seeing. I left, the next morning, believing that Budapest is one of the most beautiful cities that I have ever seen.

After landing at Heathrow, it was just a matter of hiring two cars and heading for home, eventually arriving back at Penryn during the early hours, tired but thankful.

Once refreshed, it's my usual practice to take time out and reflect on all the happenings over the previous month or so. Again, much had been achieved, new relationships had made and many situations had been overcome. Prayers had been answered and our God had been glorified.

Not long after I arrived home, the phone rang. A man from Budapest wanted to talk to me. He was an Englishmen, doing similar kind of work as myself, and he was in need of some physical help on a building project in a place called Baia Mures, about 150 miles north of Dezna. We had a chat about what was involved, and I promised to put out some feelers and see what I could come up with.

A few days later I got another call. This time it was from Paul, the young man who came to Dezna with me in August. The August trip was Paul's first time to Romania, and as this was his gap year he wanted to cram as much into it as he could. Although Dezna was physically challenging for him, he did enjoy the whole experience; so much so, he asked if I could fix him up with another trip. Now I asked myself…

"Is this God at work again?"

I told Paul about the project in Baia Mures and what was involved. One of the conditions of this particular trip was that he had to get to Budapest under his own steam, paying whatever expenses necessary.

Once there he would be picked up, taken to the site, accommodation would be provided, but he had to buy his own food. I estimated that the whole trip would cost about £400.

Paul said, "I don't have any money. What should I do?"

I suggested that he wrote out a C.V. for himself, explaining what it was all about, that this would be his second trip to Romania that year, that he was a student in a gap year, and that he wanted to use this time helping others. With that done he was encouraged to hawk it around Falmouth, especially with the small traders. Starting off with nothing, this had to be a 'no lose' situation. Paul agreed.

Four days later, Paul came back and said, "Bryan, I have £400, my flight is booked and I'm off on Friday."

Up went the cry, "Praise the Lord!"

The following Monday he was actually on the site working. From the first phone call to actually being on the site took less than two weeks.

That's my God at work!

And so operation Dezna rolled on. Another trip to Dezna and we had the water laid on, the central heating and plumbing finished on the first two floors, although the top floor was still to be done. This was a giant step forward and a great deal of thanks have to go to Chris and Ben, two young stalwart volunteers who contributed enormously to that achievement. Again it must be said, these two lads were not committed Christians, but oh, that we could have more like them! Commitment and hard work was the order of the day. Tremendous initiative was shown and a good productive attitude. These two were an answer to prayer.

Chris and Ben couldn't stay for the full duration of our time, their having to leave after two and a half weeks and return to their jobs back home. Before they left I gathered everyone around the table and had a specific time of prayer just for them. I truly felt that our prayerful concern was greatly appreciated by them both. Moreover I got the impression that they had never been the subject of prayer before, and the look on their faces showed that it had registered.

With the electrics done, gas supply in, hot and cold water in the kitchen, and all three floors ready for decorating, I was in a buoyant mood. A great deal had been achieved. I also thought that with one more big push the place would be almost finished.

As usual, my job in between visits was to recruit a team for the following year, having first ascertained the skills needed. The major work left was the bathrooms and toilets, plus the drainage system.

I needed to coordinate with Gordon as to what the specific program was. I believed that with the right people on board we could almost get the project finished and make some in-roads with regards to any furniture needed: wardrobes, beds, cabinets, tables and chairs etc. The house needed to be turned into a home and now was the time to start thinking along those lines. It was no good waiting until these things were actually needed before making a start; work of this nature meant that we needed to keep thinking ahead.

A sad part of this journey was the fact that Pastor Nicu had been scheduled for heart surgery. He was a key man in this whole operation, and we needed to show some concern for him. I don't know what actually brought this about, but he led quite a frenetic lifestyle.

Looking after his flock, Casa Torch, and his family, coupled with the way he worried, the lack of sleep, the hours he spends behind the wheel, meetings with so many different departments pertaining to the building, had taken its toll. Many a time I spoke to him about it but to no avail. Now the price had to be paid. This surgery was programmed for the spring of 2003, but for whatever reason, Nicu couldn't fit that date in. Also there was the small matter of £3,500 that was needed before the surgery could go ahead. With the spring date cancelled, October 2003 was pencilled in. That date in turn was cancelled, because the doctor had gone to Germany, and there was no one else to perform the surgery. End of October and I rang Adina, Nicu's wife. She told me that Nicu was in bed poorly, not due to his heart but just feeling generally washed out.

Looking at the bigger picture, I didn't believe the situation conducive to consider surgery at that moment in time. Nicu needed to enter such a situation in the best possible physical condition and he needed all his powers of recuperation to make a speedy and full recovery.

It was winter time in Romania, which meant freezing conditions and a lot of snow. All building work ceased, with many roads blocked by snow. Nicu was limited as to what he could do or where he could go. That could only be good news. Maybe it was God's way of giving him the leisure time he needed.

I encouraged people at Emmanuel to sustain this man in prayer. A new year began; Christmas and New Year had passed by and it was time to start planning for this year's trip to Dezna. A recruitment drive was the usual first step, and the hardest. To get the right men, with the right skills, and all be able to get the right time off from their respective employers always takes some doing, but I've always managed it in the past and, being the eternal optimist, had high hopes this year too. So, early January, out came my pen and paper, and with that, telephones started to ring.

Chris, our central heating man, having worked in Romania before his involvement in our work in Dezna, had a name for me - a man called Paul (the name alone encouraged me). This man had also worked in Romania, doing volunteer work of a similar nature. I felt this was important as he would know what to expect with regards to the work practices and frustrations. The other good news was that Paul didn't live too far from me. So a meeting was arranged, and an in-depth conversation took place. The result was that I came away very encouraged. Paul was still active in the building trade and had a few contacts with men who had the various skills needed for that stage of the project. He promised to put out a few feelers and get back to me.

Feeling encouraged I put my mind to work and came up with a work program for the next visit to Dezna. I shared the good news with Gordon Temple, which I'm sure put a big smile on his face. So, dates and duration of trip agreed, we started to think about fund raising. In the past I'd the use of a mini bus from Torch but circumstances in Leicester meant that I didn't have that option now and to hire a suitable vehicle to accommodate all our needs was going to cost about £1,400. Adding that to our food bill, ferry crossing, insurances etc, I estimated that the total cost of the enterprise would be somewhere in the region of £2000 plus.

Enter Three-Milestone Social Club into the equation and, in particular, a lady names Lesley. The club arranged a social evening with the theme being 'Fund raising for Romania': raffles, quizzes and a slave market. That sounded a bit ominous but was actually quite fun. What happens is that someone, anyone, offers themselves as a 'slave' to perform a task. It could be to wash your car for a month, do your ironing for two weeks, make a dinner for four people, do a week's housework, or baby-sitting. To turn these offers into money, one had to make a bid, as at an auction. This proved to be very effective, very productive and a fun time. It also meant that everyone was in some way involved in the project. On that one particular evening over £1000 was raised. In the past, recruiting volunteers and fund raising had always been hard work. Doing things this way was not only easier and more effective but enjoyable as well. Again I felt that…

God was at work.

Team chosen, dates set, ferry crossing booked, insurances in place, we turned our attention to the tools needed and to the materials that we felt that we were to take with us. Space on the bus was a crucial factor, meaning that we had to plan carefully and not double up or take unnecessary tools. The bus was not only going to be a means of transport. It had to serve as our home for the two or three days' journey. Therefore a degree of comfort was essential.

The team: Paul, Chris, Steve, Mike, Alec, Allan, Edgy and myself were in most part strangers to each other, so the whole situation was going to be a learning process. I also thought that it was going to be an interesting experience and one that I looked forward to.

A note on the man Edgy: here was a full-grown married man who had never been out of Cornwall in his life. He was very apprehensive about the whole business, and it was thought that he might even pull out at the last minute. I was praying that this would not happen, as I had a certain 'peace' about the way things had developed. I also believed that this whole experience was going to have a lasting effect on the lives of these men. More about Edgy later!

As time spent on site was limited, it was important that we had continuity and not be held up for any reason. To enable that, it was decided that the best thing for me to do would be to fly out to Dezna ahead of the team and prepare things in readiness: materials, accommodation, food etc.

So one week before Easter, I set off alone on the overnight train from Truro. This got me into Reading at about 4.30 am, which meant an hour and a half wait in a deserted station until the bus that took me to Heathrow arrived. At 6 o'clock, I left for the airport. After a forty minute drive I arrived at terminal 2, and had another five-hour wait until flight time. This gave me time to have a wash and freshen myself up. Then it was breakfast, a newspaper, then settling down and waiting. I find airports interesting places; people of all shapes and sizes pass by, some with just a newspaper tucked under their arm, others with trolley loads of luggage, people of every nation, culture and colour, all travelling to all parts of the globe and for various reasons, and Heathrow is just one of many such places.

A five-hour flight, Heathrow to Bucharest, allowing for the time difference, then change of flights and a one and a half hour flight from Bucharest to Timisoara. That was the plan, but on arriving in Bucharest at 4 pm, their time, we were told that all Romanian flights were cancelled due to the pilots being on strike. Reporting to the information desk, we were told that the final incoming flight for that day would be about 9 o'clock. Once all onward travelling passengers were together, buses would be laid on for the onward journey, and in my case, Bucharest to Timisoara would leave at 9.30 pm and take nine hours to arrive.

Considering my overnight train journey from Truro to Heathrow, this meant a second night without proper sleep. I was not best pleased. Not only that, Nicu would be waiting at Timisoara to pick me up and wouldn't know of the arrangements that had to be made. Somehow I had to contact him. Thankfully a fellow passenger let me use his mobile phone, and another passenger, a young Romanian girl who spoke English, came to my rescue.

Nicu was contacted, and alternative arrangements were made satisfying everyone's need. At six the following morning, I was greeted by the smiling Nicu and Adina outside the Continental hotel, Timisoara. Another two-hour drive saw us arrive in Dezna. Five minutes later and I was in bed, where I slept deeply for about eight hours.

The following weekend was the start of Easter, and Thursday night all shops and businesses closed until the following Tuesday. As the next day was Wednesday, I didn't have much time to shop for the necessary materials. The team arrived sometime on Sunday, so I had a lot to do. Arad was where we did most of the buying, and it was about 90 km away. Again forward planning came to my rescue. The previous year I had the good sense to buy some materials that might be needed the following year, so whenever the men would arrive we would already have some materials on site that would enable them to get on with things.

Sunday came and I had the water laid on, heating working, beds all made and some food in the larder. With the kettle on the boil, all was ready.

Praise the Lord!

Sunday, mid-afternoon, and the men arrived; they had a long drive, 1,600 miles and no proper sleep. All were quite tired, but, as I have experienced, excitement and curiosity overcame tiredness, and all wanted to see the building and what was expected from them. None were disappointed.

Nicu came around and was introduced. After that it was a matter of unloading the considerable amount of tools and materials, finding a home for everything and preparing a meal. With no women with us, our menu was pretty basic and somewhat haphazard, but there was a good attitude all round. Personal comfort was second on our list of priorities, the work being the first.

Easter is an important time on the Romanian calendar, and it is taken very seriously; so much so that Nicu came round that evening and said that it would be frowned on if any work was done before the Tuesday. If work was done it would reflect badly on him as a minister. I explained this to the men but as non-Christians they were a little perplexed. I suspect that Easter and its significance meant little to them, plus the sole purpose of their visit was to work. Nevertheless they agreed, but only in part, as there were things that could be done (and which could be done quietly) as we were working behind closed doors. No one needed to know. I agreed. Eight men at twelve hours a day for three days would have meant the loss of 288 hours work. With so much to do, we just couldn't afford to lose that amount of time, and what Nicu didn't know couldn't hurt him. I think in this case the end justified the means.

It was during this quiet time that things took a turn for the worse, and I felt that I was put in a position whereby I had to defend my Christian principles. One of the men, the carpenter, no names needed, decided to go and explore the local bars, ending up spending most of the day in one. The result was that he came back quite drunk. Word soon got back that he was flashing a lot of money around and buying some of the locals drink. This was not a wise thing to do and flashing money about was asking for trouble. It also reflected badly on the Englishmen. The other men responded angrily and wanted him out of the accommodation and off the site. Getting drunk on day two meant that he was no good to us on day three either, and as a team we all needed each other's skills to operate smoothly.

Strong words were spoken to the man concerned and he apologised to everyone. I then had to speak with the team to see if the apology was enough to restore the peace. Sadly it wasn't, the men saying that they couldn't forgive him or his behaviour. I expressed my disappointment with them, stating that I believed it was more a case of wouldn't rather than couldn't and that I was very disappointed.

Eventually there was some relenting, and it was said that they would carry on, but only doing it for my sake. I told of my appreciation for their decision, and the situation was diffused. Unfortunately it all proved to be a waste of time as the following day the man concerned got a telephone message telling him that his mother had died, and once again he sought solace in the bar. So the incident was repeated, this time with the chippie being literally carried back to the accommodation and being put to bed, early in the evening. This time the men had no hesitation; they just collected all his belongings and threw everything out of the building, stating that they didn't want to associate with him. Later the chippie got up and went out.

I was genuinely concerned for this man as the days at that time of the year were quite warm but the nights were freezing, as much as 10 below, and not a time to be without a warm place to sleep. This, and being in a state of intoxication, was likely to lead to a dangerous and fatal situation. I felt obliged to go and collect all this man's belongings and make a bed for him in my room.

By now news of this situation had spread through the town. Nicu came to see me and together we went searching for this man. We found him in a bar and tried to persuade him to return to his room. He refused, saying that he wouldn't mix with the men or they with him. I said that he could sleep in my room and that that was where all his belongings were, as I had collected them and put there. Again he refused.

I suggested to Nicu that we take our leave and just let things develop. Once away from everyone, Nicu and I offered the situation to the Lord, praying that the bar would be vacated and peace restored. I then said to Nicu that having prayed the prayer we should not continue to worry about things, as that would indicate a lack of trust in the good Lord. That done Nicu went home and I to my room.

I decided to make myself a drink before retiring and made my way to the kitchen. It was there that I bumped into one of the team. By now all knew of my decision to give the chippie some bed space in my room, and he let it be known that this had not met with their approval and that they couldn't understand my attitude. I explained that my Christian principles wouldn't allow me to see a fellow human being turfed out of his room, to spend the night outside in freezing conditions, and that I would take the same attitude for any of the team, no matter what.

He mellowed a little, and responded by saying, "I believe you would." He added that I had a way of affecting people's lives.

I took that as a great compliment and as confirmation that decisions I'd made were the right ones. There was no bad feeling at all, just a different way of responding to a situation, and I think that he learnt more than I did.

Praise the Lord!

Drink in hand I returned to my room, intending to go straight to bed, but once again God was at work, and in walked the chippie. This was only ten or fifteen minutes after the prayers had been said. I felt that this was a heaven-sent opportunity to have a talk with this man on a one-to-one basis. I demanded that he sit down. I think that my attitude told him that I was in no mood to be challenged and he sat down.

I then asked him, "What is your problem?" saying that within thirty-six hours of arrival he had, on two occasions upset the whole team, plus Nicu and me, stained our reputation in the village, and frustrated the work program.

His reply was that he was upset because of the death of his mother. I countered by saying that I just didn't believe him, because some of this obnoxious behaviour had taken place before he had heard about his mother. He objected to being called a liar, and we were locked eyeball to eyeball.

After a very short while he seemed to deflate, giving out a great sigh; then he started to talk. He told me that he had been very close to his dad and that not long ago his dad had died and that he had taken it very hard. His sister, who was fourteen years younger than him, also took it hard and became very depressed, almost suicidal. He, being the eldest child, felt that he needed to take care of his sister, which wasn't easy for him. Added to that, he was in the middle of a divorce, had recently lost his job and now learnt his mother had died. He then cried. I have to confess that at that moment my attitude towards this man changed and the Jesus in me came to the fore. I also believed that all this was a part of God's answer to our prayers and that this situation had to be developed.

I told this man how much I sympathised with him, but despite all he would not find any answers in a bottle. In looking in the bottle he was only bringing shame and disgrace to the family name; if he loved his parents as much as he said he did, he should have a desire to honour them with his behaviour and not bring shame. Also, if his sister was looking to him for support, she was hardly going to get it if he was continually drunk. That would only be making matters worse, letting her down in the process.

I asked him if he still loved his wife.

He said, "Yes."

I asked him if he talked to his wife and he said, "No."

I suggested that the first thing he had to do when he got home was to sit down and start talking, to put an end to the divorce proceedings and not be too surprised if he found out his wife felt the same way as he did, then find employment. That shouldn't be too difficult for a carpenter. With regards to the passing of his mum and dad, that was something he just had to come to terms with. I explained that death was inevitable to us all, but as a Christian one could find a peace about these things. I went on to emphasize that his chosen route for dealing with all this would only make matters worse and that he would be wise to rethink the whole situation.

This conversation lasted about an hour, and I felt it right to bring it to a close and not overstate things. It was then that this man asked if I would pray for him.

I said, "No!"

He looked at me quite shocked, but I went on to explain that as he recognised that there is a God to pray to, he could pray himself. God is available to everyone and He would want this man to call on Him, at any time and for any reason. So I suggested that we each got into our own bed and turned out the lights. He could just lie there and quietly pray - not only pray but believe also. One of the reasons that this man had been notified about his mother was because he was needed back home to take care of the funeral arrangements, so the following day he was driven to Timisoara airport. I wished him well and waved him goodbye. I have not seen him since.

I reflected back on the recent events, and recalled that I had only left home a week before, yet so much had happened. It had been a testing time for my endurance, my patience, and spiritual discernment, and as the end result had turned out quite well, I could only say,

Praise the Lord!

With the chippie now gone, I took over his tasks. The other team members recognised the situation, and all responded accordingly. This was a good team; everyone settled down and just got on with the job.

The bathrooms, toilets, drains and laundry room were the main priority this time, plus finishing off the central heating, all of which I felt was well within the capability of this team, especially as 90% of all the materials were already on site.

Paul and Edgy took on the drainage system, Mike and Steve took on the bathrooms and toilets, Chris and Alec the central heating, and I tackled the laundry room. The place was a hive of industry.

For the laundry room there was a space at the end of the passage in the old part of the building which was perfect in size (about 10 feet square) but there was no ceiling and no windows. The floor was about six feet below the desired level, and the existing walls were made of mud brick. The whole structure needed to be demolished, footings dug and concreted, new walls built, incorporating a window, new floor shuttered and concreted, the walls timber-lined and plaster boarded, and a new ceiling put in. I took it on myself to do the demolition work, dig the footings, place the concrete and do the block work. Good planning and good cooperation resulted in the job being completed with time to spare.

Nicu paid us regular visits and was pleased with what he saw. Nicu and I also paid a visit to Viora, the site engineer. It was wise to keep her informed, as we needed her co-operation and she had a responsibility for the site. Over the years I had built up a good rapport with her. She trusted me, and I didn't want to spoil that relationship.

Shortly after 6am each day, bleary-eyed workers would begin to appear, the first port of call being the kitchen for a much-needed cuppa. By 7 o'clock all were hard at work, breaking off as-and-when for breakfast, then back on site until lunch, lunch being a sandwich or a cuppa-soup. We finished the day's work between 6.30pm and 8.00pm, had a shower and a beer, then off to the local restaurant for a nice evening meal. (A two course meal with a bottle of wine cost less than five pounds and it rounded the day off very well). Everyone was usually tucked up by 11 o'clock - all except Edgy. He was the man who had never been out of Cornwall before, the man who some thought might pull out before we left. He really was apprehensive about it all. I also said that I believed that this experience would make an impression on their lives. Well, I believe that it had, but none more than Edgy.

Sometimes, whilst others were chatting or having a drink, or even sometimes when all had gone to bed, Edgy would just sit and look at the view, even in the dark. It was when it was dark that frogs started to perform, thousands and thousands of them, all croaking away in unison. With hardly any traffic, the silence was deafening and helped to amplify the frog chorus. With a bright moon shining and stars out, Edgy thought this was as good as it got. To say that he was enthralled is to put it mildly.

I've sat with him in the dark, asking, "What are you looking at?"

With a wave of his arm he would proclaim, "This. It's wonderful. I'm coming back!" He would say, "They are lovely people. It's a lovely place and helping to provide a home for blind orphans is great, plus the beer is cheap!"

In addition to all that he had fallen in love with the waitress at the local restaurant.

Edgy was a character, always cheerful, hard working, always willing to help. Nothing was too much trouble. His language made one's ears burn. but I thought that that was a small price to pay. All work and no play is no good, and this was a beautiful country with a lot of history behind it

Timisoara, the place where the revolution started, was often mentioned, and all were curious to see it, so come Sunday we piled into the bus for a day out. Timisoara was a two-hour drive and it was a nice hot day. Revolution Square was packed with visitors, all in their Sunday best. A visit to the church was a must. It dominated one end of the square, whilst the opera house dominated the other. Between the two, and on either side, were shops and restaurants. The centre was decorated by ornamental gardens.

At about 1pm we decided to sample the local fare and settled for an open-air meal and a cool beer. Meal over, it was decided that it was time to make tracks for Dezna. Chris, who was driving, missed our turn-off, resulting in a grand tour of the countryside, travelling on some roads which would have given a tank a hard time. This also meant that we went through some quite remote villages, very primitive but very interesting.

About 7pm saw us back in camp. It was time for a shower, a cold beer, then off to the restaurant for the evening meal. After another unsuccessful attempt by Edgy to get the waitress to marry him we all went back to camp, and so to bed - a good day.

Time rolled along and it was getting close to our departure date. As usual Nicu was asking if we couldn't stay longer. Sadly the answer was, "No." These men had jobs and families to go back to. I had to explain to Nicu that working in Romania wouldn't pay the mortgage. He reluctantly understood, but every year I had the same parting conversation. As usual I felt sad for him, not only because we were parting, but because we both knew that the job would virtually come to a standstill in my absence. There was little that I could do about that. But the good news was that the place was almost ready for occupation and I had already had a plan in my mind with regard to the finishing touches that were needed.

The following day was to be our last day, so this day was all about packing up our tools and belongings, locking away all the materials that were still on site and making the place secure. That night we dined at the local restaurant and Nicu and Adina were our guests. During the meal I felt the need to tell of my appreciation for all that had been achieved, and the way of showing my appreciation to all was to pay for the meal, not too magnanimous a gesture considering the cost involved. Another enjoyable time followed, with Edgy making one last effort to marry the waitress. He failed.

I had to be at Timisoara airport the next morning by 6am, and as previously stated it was a two hour drive, which meant that I had to be up and ready about 3.30. It was an uneventful drive to the airport, goodbyes were said, and I left Romania. The Romanian National Airline is Tarom, and for internal flights they use small propeller driven planes, always full and very cramped. A drink and savoury was served which was very welcome. Then we flew off towards Bucharest, passing over the snow-capped Carpathian mountains. They presented a magnificent vista in the early morning sun.

After checking that all the team had arrived home safely, I thought that a meeting with Gordon Temple and Michael Townsend was necessary. So Sylvia and I decided to spend a weekend at Torch House to discuss the way forward with regards to Dezna.

With all the heavy work done and everything in working order, all that was left was the decorating and one or two bits of carpentry. I felt I couldn't justify another team of builders, coupled with the costs involved. Both agreed to this. Mike also said that his brother-in-law wanted to be involved with Dezna in some way. So Mike said that he would put out some feelers to that end.

A week later and Mike made contact with me saying that his brother-in-law was keen to put a small team together and make the trip to Dezna. So, with the decorating done and everything in working order, I considered my work and time in Dezna to be over. It was six years from start to finish and had been a tremendous challenge. Much had been overcome.

Considering the way that it had been done, I believe that a mountain had been climbed. It had been a tremendous challenge, testing my patience, resilience, commitment, strength, and judgment, but whenever the going got tough, I just reminded myself and Sylvia about those who would be benefiting from all this, some of the visually impaired, orphaned children of Romania - those who were not in a position to help themselves, those who were put in this position by man. Therefore God had deemed that man should help redeem this situation. I was pleased and privileged that I had been chosen as one of them.

Since leaving Dezna, dear Nicu had been into hospital and had his heart surgery. He was now home and under strict orders to have a complete rest, both in mind and body. I hoped he'd act sensibly, and he did just that. Just two of the many lasting memories of my time spent in Dezna are:

1). After watching the local football team play one Sunday and noticing their rather tatty strip, it was thought that maybe we could do something about it. So during one of our discussions with the men it was decided that we would buy a new football strip for the village team. Having watched them play in the past and knowing that there was a home game being played on our last Sunday, we all went to the match and cheered them on. After the match was over we went into their dressing room and handed over the new strip. They were quite amazed and thrilled; so much so that we were invited to the local pub to celebrate their victory (they won 3-1) and their new strip, plus the making of new friends. It was drinks all round and all agreed that it was a good day. This is a good way of breaking down barriers, crossing cultures, and making friends.

2). On one our trips Sylvia and I were given a large quantity of quality toys, diggers, cars, trains, tractors etc. When we packed our car, I said that we had to put these toys in last, so as to have easy access to them. We also prayed that God would highlight just whom we should give these toys to. Having a consistent God I felt sure that he would point out who the recipient of these toys would be, and I would need to be able to put my hands on them straight away. I had travelled many miles and always with the toys on the back seat. As yet I had not felt prompted to part with them. In all my years of travel for the Lord I had always trusted that He would point the finger and be my guide, as and when necessary, and as yet, with regard to the toys, nothing.

With the car checked over and packed, with our 'goodbye's said, we had an early night. With such a long journey ahead, experience had taught me that an early start is essential, especially as the first part of the journey was in Romania, where the roads were the poorest, and therefore the slowest. At about 6.30 and with dawn just breaking, we set off at a slow pace, going through many little villages. It was as we passed through one such village that I first saw them - two little boys. I guessed one to be about four or five, the other a little older, maybe six. There was not another living soul in sight, just these two little chaps walking hand in hand by the side of the road.

I instinctively cried out to Sylvia, "There they are! They are the ones who I must give the toys to!" They were highlighted in the glare of my headlights - just what I had prayed for. I drove past them about fifty feet, stopped the car and got out. They were now facing me. They saw me looking at them and they stopped walking. With either a quizzical or concerned look on their faces, they just stood there. I took the bag of toys from the back seat, and holding the bag out in front of me, slowly walked towards them. Once up to them I opened the bag and offered it to them. My big regret was that I didn't have my camera with me. Seeing their faces when they looked in the bag was worth more than a thousand words could say. The eldest boy put his hand in the bag and took out a single toy. The younger one started to do the same. I stopped him, made the other boy put the toy back in the bag. I then took his hand and made him grip the handle of the bag, offering the other handle to the other boy. That done I shooed them away. They didn't believe what was happening. They stood there for a short while, the elder of the two pointed to the bag and then pointed to himself. I nodded, and said, "Da" (yes). Slowly they turned and walked away, talking excitedly, looking in the bag, and turning around to look at me all at the same time. I actually felt their joy. The whole episode only took two or three minutes, but the memory, for all concerned, would last a lifetime.

God was at work!

Once home it was just a matter of pulling the plug on the phone and hibernating for three or four days. Obviously being away for so long, a stack of mail awaited us - most of it junk and all of which I pushed to one side; another day or two for that wouldn't hurt. I checked things out around the property and everything was fine. God had answered our prayers. As was usual it took four or five days for us to get back to normal. Fortunately both of us, being retired, had the time. Once fully rested, our body clocks back to normal, we were back into our old routine.

With the mail sorted, the grass cut, larder replenished, it was time to catch up on our thoughts; where we had come from with this work and where did we go from here.

We make a living

By what we get

We make a life

By what we give

PREJMER

After being home for several weeks and feeling fully recovered, a certain restlessness came over me. There was now something missing in my life. In my heart of hearts I already knew what it was. I had lost a certain purpose, a certain need to get up in the morning. My work in Dezna and Valea Crisului wasn't just about packing up the car and going out to do the job. It was also about the planning, the organising, fund raising, the recruitment drive and the anticipation of it all. All this took quite some time to bring together and kept me busy, both physically and mentally. In other words, there was a big void in my life, and I needed it filled.

So what was I to do? The first thing I did do was to talk with Sylvia. After spending 46 years together she already knew my mind and my heart. We committed it all to God. I've always believed that it is not enough to believe in God. One has to also trust in God too, so having prayed about this, I sat back and awaited developments. They were not long in coming.

It was only a matter of days when I was in contact with a man named Damien. Damien lived in the Birmingham area and was in need of some help to renovate a building in a place called Prejmer. When this place was finished it would be home for twelve or more infants. This to me was very good news because it meant the children would be starting their lives growing up in a loving environment virtually from day one and would not become institutionalised in their early and formative years, which in itself would have created a major problem.

After some dialogue with Damien, a picture of the situation started to evolve in my mind - part of it good, part not so good. Many years experience working in Romania had taught me not to take things at face value. There seemed to be a lot going on here but with a lot of loose ends attached, and some of the information was somewhat conflicting. Again, after a chat with Sylvia I decided that there would be a lot to gain if I went to Prejmer and evaluated the whole situation for myself.

Sylvia agreed, so I started to make my travel arrangements for what was turning out to be the next step on my journey with the Lord.

After consulting my map, I saw that Prejmer was situated about fifteen miles northwest of Brasov, which was on the eastern side of Romania. It was also about 350 miles beyond were I normally would have turned off for Dezna, which in turn meant that it was an extra day's drive, so I decided that my best option was to fly. And it was here that I encountered the first situation that I had to deal with.

For reasons that are beyond me, the cheap airlines like Ryanair and Easyjet did not fly into Bucharest, the capital of Romania, but they did fly to Budapest, which was the capital of Hungary. The journey from Budapest to Brasov took several hours. Also, because of my time of arrival at the airport, it meant that I would be faced with another night's travel and with an additional cost. To fly direct to Bucharest I needed to go by a scheduled B.A. flight, which again was more expensive than Ryanair or Easyjet, but the time saved made it worthwhile.

As with Dezna, I now found myself going into a situation somewhat blindly. This was history repeating itself. I had never been to Brasov before. I didn't know anyone there, and as yet, I had no accommodation waiting for me.

This was a situation not lost on Sylvia who asked me, "What are you going to do when you get to Bucharest?"

"I don't know," I said, "but if this is God's work then we just have to trust Him."

Having already booked my flight we didn't have much option. That, plus the scripture, told me God would supply all my needs (Philippians 4 v 19).

I figured that, as God made these promises, I, as a Christian, have the right to claim and make use of them. As I said to the children in Emmanuel Church, "It's not enough to believe in God. We have to put our trust in Him also."

Enter the Cleaford Trust. This is a web site set up by a certain John Cleaford, and its function was to publish and distribute an informative news sheet, essentially for volunteers who worked in Romania. It was here that people could share their needs and pass on information about the ever changing rules and regulations in Romania, and it was here that I let it be known about my needs with regards to my intended trip to Brasov.

A week later and I got an email from someone giving me an email address of a man in Brasov who provided a service that would meet my need. Daniel Hristia was a Romanian man who had set up a charity to help the gypsy children in the Brasov area. He provided a bus service, which helped to raise funds for this work. This was good news. Daniel helped me, I helped him, and we both helped the children - brilliant! This was God's promise becoming a reality.

Two days later and I got a phone call from Damien in Birmingham. He knew about my intended trip and offered me free use of a flat that he owned in Brasov but with the one proviso, namely that I was to be out of the flat by the 25th of October. Surprise, surprise - my return flight was on the 25th of October, and that had been booked nearly a month before. God was keeping His promise. But I asked how to get into the flat and where the key was. Damien gave me an email address of Andra, a young lady, who looked after the flat. I emailed Andra, and between us we arranged the time and meeting place for the handing over of the key.

The day arrived when I found myself arriving in Bucharest, there to be met by Daniel, a man who I had never met before. He took me to Brasov where I was met by Andra, a lady that I had also never met before. She gave me the keys to a flat belonging to a man I have never met. With Daniel promising to pick me up on the morning of the 25th, I can truly say that this was my God at work meeting all my needs as promised. This was not only encouraging for me but also gave Sylvia peace of mind.

My plan was to spend a week in Brasov, to see what was on the agenda work-wise, the materials needed and the availability of such materials. I have said many times before that forward planning was essential in this work; it saved precious time and money, both crucial elements in volunteer work. Andra, the young lady who met me at the flat, said that she would be happy to help me during my stay. She was almost fluent in English and obviously knew her way around town, and this proved to be a great help to me. Once rested, we arranged to go out to Prejmer, there to meet Jan, the American lady, who (I believe) set up the charity. With Jan was a Romanian man called

Florin. He apparently oversaw the work that went on there in Prejmer, and thankfully he also spoke good English.

Prejmer was the name of the village in which this property was situated. The charity was called Casa Mea (My House). Casa Mea was, in part, in quite a good state of repair, with a lot of work already done. The downstairs kitchen and bathrooms were 90% complete, but the bedrooms needed complete renovation. The ceilings, walls, and floors needed attention, then decorating. In addition to this work, two new bathrooms needed to be installed on the first floor. On this, my first visit, I only spent an hour or so. Jan, who had a small child with her, had to leave early. So I made an arrangement with Florin to pick me up early the following day. Then, armed with a tape, calculator, paper and pen, and with the whole day at our disposal, we went into a lot of detail.

It's about a half hour drive from Brasov to the town of Prejmer, and with just Florin and myself in the car it gave us a chance to have a chat about what had gone on in the past with regards to the work in Casa Mea. I got the impression from Damien that he had been involved in this work from the start. I learnt that he had only made one visit to Casa Mea, and the trip had been treated more as a holiday than a works project, with limited hours actually being put in on the site. This, I find, is one of the difficulties with volunteers, but when people are prepared to give up their time and make the effort to travel to Romania to help others, how can one criticise how they use their time?

I believe that it was all a matter of attitude. I went out to work with a bit of leisure time thrown in. Others went out for leisure time with a bit of work thrown in. From the start I felt that there were some loose ends and conflicting statements being made. Now things started to fall into place. Damien and his team had only stayed one week, and they stayed in Brasov for that time, which meant that commuting daily to and from Prejmer took up a fair amount of time. Again, experience taught me that this was not a good working practice. The difference between being on site at 7.00 am and 9.00 or 9.30, multiplied between eight or nine people added up to a lot of missed working hours - not good news.

Florin seemed an amiable chap, but being a Romanian I reserved my final judgment until I got to know him better. Before we went to Casa Mea, Florin took me to his home, where I met his wife and parents. They made me welcome by providing coffee and pumpkin. There was an open water course flowing across the yard, and that was where the pumpkins were kept, in the open but submerged in water. It helped keep them cool and fresh, a sort of open air fridge - Romanian style.

It was here that I asked Florin about accommodation. I always had a concern for Sylvia. I wanted her to enjoy our work in Romania and not have to rough it in any way. Florin's home consisted of a kitchen, bathroom and living-cum-bedroom area - very small but very nice and tastefully done.

Florin said that he and his wife would happily move into his brother's house, and Sylvia and I could stay in Florin's. This to me was a very good arrangement. Sylvia would be happy there, and it was literally just round the corner from where I would be working. Naturally I paid Florin for this kindness, so everyone benefited.

Coffee drunk, pumpkin eaten and then it was round to Casa Mea. Florin brought me up to date with the history of Casa Mea and the work that had gone on in the past. Sadly it was the same old story - start and stop, start and stop. I had to accept the fact that this was the way it would always be when volunteers were involved. All works, be it Valea Crisului, Dezna or Casa Mea were big projects. They took a considerable amount of time to complete, and time spent on site by volunteers was limited. However, I did believe that with a proper strategy and good planning, better and quicker progress could be made.

Looking at the overall building, I saw it as three separate projects. At one end of the building was a long room: eight feet ceiling height, forteen metres long and five metres wide. The plan was to turn it into a laundry room, a bathroom and two bedrooms, plus a stairwell for access to the first floor.

I suggested to Florin that the best thing to do would be to first plasterboard the ceiling, then dry-line the walls using 4x2 studwork, plasterboard finish, with insulation in behind; then to put up the partitions and door linings, tile the floors, with all the electrics going in, as and when. Doing things this way was much quicker than sand and cement render (wet work). It was also much warmer, which was a vital factor out there considering the winter temperatures and, I believe, a cheaper way of doing things, which was another important consideration. I pointed out that with five good men I could complete the works during my spring visit to Prejmer. Florin now had a big smile on his face.

So, it was on to Phase 2 of Casa Mea. Going to the other end of the building, we had the office and, below that, the boiler room. I suggested the same procedure for the interior of the office, with a second team of four men (volunteers) taking on this work. This also could be completed during the spring visit. Whilst both of these phases were going on, the exterior of the office and boiler room could be sand and cement rendered by a local team of Romanians, and all this work could be going on simultaneously. Florin's smile got wider.

The next part of the work needed to be well planned. The bedrooms on the first floor had low-ish ceilings. To remedy this meant stripping off the roof, raising the surrounding walls by nearly one metre and replacing the roof. Because this was all outside work it meant, essentially, a summertime job. It also meant that it had to be started and finished in one go - no stopping and starting. Another consideration was that there was a lot of completed work beneath the roof. Also the necessary funds needed to be in place for the work to happen, and Jan had led me to believe that funds were tight. I advised Jan to go back to the States and get her fellow trustees to start fund raising.

Fortunately, at that moment in time, Jan had the time to do this. Jan was going through a learning process here, realising that it was often a three steps forward and two steps back situation. It was very frustrating, but one had to learn to live with it. Keeping focused on the end result always helped me - the end result being the children who would have a proper home here.

Come mid-afternoon, I had just about figured out all that I needed to know about Casa Mea. So now I turned my attention to the materials needed, the costs involved, and where to get them. Florin came up with the name "Practiker", which turned out to be a Homebase type of superstore with just about everything that would be needed. With all the prices displayed, it proved to be quite easy to put a cost on everything, plus, they had a delivery service. Things were looking up. I had never had this luxury before and prayers were being answered.

That done we were off to the wood-mill to check on all the studwork needed. This meant a forty minute drive in Florin's car along one of the worst Romanian roads I had ever been on. 5 mph was the maximum speed possible, but we did go through some interesting places, and the slow speed meant that I had time to look around and see things: the snow-capped mountains in the background, for instance, wild flowers, and the ever-changing landscape. I also got to see the natives at work.

Having arrived at the mill, Florin assured me that this man gave value for money and the product was good. What I was looking for was straight, dry timber, and size consistency, all of which I was assured of. It was whilst I was there that I noticed three boys of various ages, ranging from four or five to about ten or twelve (I had always found it difficult to assess the age of children out there, because they were so under-nourished and under-developed.) They were filling large sacks of sawdust. I asked Florin what was going on. He explained that, as with any wood mill, there was always a great deal of sawdust produced as a by-product, and as it was difficult to get rid of, the local gypsies were allowed to send their children to take whatever they needed. This, he told me, was spread over the floor of their home and provided a degree of warmth and some insulation, the alternative being just a dirt floor, which would be cold and damp. These three boys were going to have to carry these sacks about a mile and a half. So, rather than see them struggle, Florin and I put them and the sacks into the car and drove them home. This act of kindness also meant that I found myself in the heart of the gypsy community. As I wrote early on in my story, in Romania you have the poor, the very poor, and then the gypsies. The squalor in the gypsy areas was unbelievable unless seen with one's own eyes. It's hard to believe that in this, the 21st century, people actually lived like that. This wasn't the first time that I had found myself in this situation but it was still a shock, and I couldn't get away quick enough.

With the site visited, the job sussed out and with a strategy in mind, the materials seen and some costing done, the accommodation sorted, I now felt that this trip had proved to be well worthwhile. Now I needed to go and visit Jan and give her my assessment of the whole situation.

Jan owned her own rented apartment in Brasov. Not knowing where it was, I made contact with Andra, and after a phone call to Jan, we set off by bus to pay her a visit. It was only a ten-minute ride but I enjoyed doing things in a way that let me integrate myself into the local community, plus it was a lot cheaper than a taxi.

I outlined my thoughts to Jan about Casa Mea, the 'how', the 'why', and the 'when', also giving a realistic appraisal of the costs involved. Jan was encouraged by this and gave it her seal of approval.

It was here that Jan went into some detail about the difficulties that she had had to deal with, whilst getting Casa Mea up and running. Considering the fact that this lady was there on her own and had to cope with her adopted child, I think that she had done remarkably well, but secretly, I questioned the wisdom of the situation. This lady was out of her depth and needed help. Perhaps this was where I came in - who knows?

All things considered, this had been a worthwhile trip. I could go home now feeling a lot more confident about the whole situation, but as I still had two days to go before my day of departure, I met up with Andra again and she acted as my guide, giving gave me a grand tour of Brasov.

The inner city itself was quite modern by Romanian standards: plush banks, posh cars, nice restaurants, trams, buses and taxis everywhere. It's an ancient city with a lot of history. A granite wall about twenty feet high surrounded the inner city, with round towers strategically placed within sight of each other. It was in Brasov where the first revolution took place in 1985. Many houses still bear the scars of that conflict, with walls being riddled with bullet holes. Andra told me that people liked to keep the scars to remind themselves of their past and of the price that had been paid for their freedom.

So, 25th of October, and it was time to leave. I said my 'goodbye's to all concerned. Daniel arrived on time and we started the four-hour drive to the airport. Before I left Penryn, Daniel had told me that the winter snows had started in Romania. Yet, when I arrived in Brasov, it was bathed in sunshine, and I enjoyed a week of glorious weather. Now, on this day, the snows had started again - perfect timing. I arrived home safe and sound. As they say, God is good.

Throughout this, my journey with the Lord, God had answered many prayers for me and none more remarkable than a more recent one. At the beginning of my journey I told of my visit to Tambov in Russia. It was there that I made friends with Gennadi and his family, plus many other people in his fellowship. However, some 14 years had passed, and for various reasons we had lost touch. This saddened me somewhat, because I do like to keep in touch with people, and I was at a loss as to what I could do about this. Letters and cards went unanswered.

Enter Kath Snelling! Kath was a member of Emmanuel many years ago, leaving to do missionary work in Russia. When on leave, Kath usually paid a visit to Emmanuel to catch up with her friends, and I told Kath about my loss of contact with Gennadi. When Kath returned to Moscow she attended a seminar there. A man stood up and gave a talk. He mentioned the name Tambov. This 'rang a bell' in Kath's mind, as she knew of my visit to Tambov.

After the talk was over Kath approached the man, and asked him, "Do you know Bryan Parr?"

He said, "Yes!"

Kath had the good sense to take some details from him and, as a result of this amazing coincidence, Gennadi and I are back in touch with one another. There are an estimated 200 million people in Russia, and out of that number of people I needed to find just one. God saw fit to bring these two people together at that time and at that place, and once again my need was met.

That's my God at work!

Back home and my mind started ticking over. I needed to think about raising funds. As usual I enjoyed the enthusiastic support of several members of Emmanuel Church. I anticipated that other members of the team would get themselves motivated. With the charity also helping out, all would be well. I don't let situations like this bother me too much. If this work was in line with God's thinking, then He was my assurance and insurance. That done, I said a covering prayer, sat back and awaited results. It was not long before a slow trickle of contributions started to come in.

Having shared the work with the fellowship, and telling of the need for things for babies and infants e.g. clothing, bedding, and cuddly toys, I was now spending much of my time collecting all the stuff. Sylvia then went through it all, as we only had a top box and the car itself. Fortunately the car was a Volvo (one could pack a great deal in such a vehicle), but we still had to be selective about what we took out with us, and I left most of that to Sylvia.

It was February, and I had started to make some enquiries about our travel arrangements: European travel insurance, personal insurance, accommodation on route, ferry crossing. As we were planning to leave on the 8th of April all this needed to be in place well in advance.

Another change to the travel arrangements was that Sylvia and I thought it best to make an early start on the Friday and, instead of having 'Bed and Breakfast' in Dover, to catch an earlier ferry, maybe get as far as Liege in Belgium and then to look for a 'Bed and Breakfast'. I believed that it would make better use of our time and get us there a bit earlier. It also meant that we would be driving across Hungary and Romania on the Sunday when most of the commercial traffic would be off the road. That way we could enjoy the drive much better.

Now it was just a matter of confirming the team and waiting. Within two weeks everything was in place and a team of ten was ready to go. The travel arrangements were such that it meant Sylvia and I arrived in Prejmer ahead of Damien and the others. On arrival we leisurely unpacked our belongings and got to know our hosts: Florin and his wife, Mahaila; Mahaila's father, Mihai; and Mahaila's mother, Nootzie. Our rooms were next to the cow-shed. The cow was with calf, the cat had just had kittens and the dog was pregnant. They seemed to keep a continuity of animals for practical reasons; the calf would be fattened up and butchered to enhance their food supply.

Tuesday, and it was time to start thinking about going to work. The first thing that I needed to do was to check what materials were on site. I was keen for Sylvia to have as much rest as possible, so I left her in bed, got my own breakfast, then walked round to the site. Three to four hundred yards or so, and I was there. This was a good arrangement for me. Being able to walk to the site meant that I didn't have to rely on anyone and I could be on site at 7am sharp, setting a good example to the others. It wasn't too long before the team arrived, and I was glad to see them.

This proved to be a good team, with many of the trades needed: decorators, electrician, tilers, and three general handymen. We were on site, with jobs allocated, and it was all stations go!

On my previous visit I had left instructions that the barn was to be cleared out in readiness for our arrival. Also much needed materials were to be on site. It was a welcome sight to see everything had been done as requested, and I expressed my thanks. The barn was fourteen metres long by five metres wide and was going to be partitioned off using stud work. When finished it would be two bedrooms, a bathroom, a laundry room, and access to a stair well that would lead up to the first floor. In addition, both the office and the barn would have considerable electrical works installed. So, jobs allocated, everyone generally supporting each other as and when needed, and a small kitchen made available to us, made for a happy time.

With everything that was needed on site, the site being close by, and putting in ten hours a day with Mihai and Florin's help, meant that good progress was made, and both Jan and the locals were quite impressed. However, soon things began to reveal themselves to me. Mihai couldn't speak a word of English and knew nothing about the construction business but was extremely enthusiastic and a willing worker. Florin, on the other hand, spoke excellent English, knew a great deal about the construction business but lacked enthusiasm and would leave the site for whatever reason. This needed to be addressed. Time was one of my biggest enemies.

So, that evening I had a little chat with Florin and things got better. I also learned that there was a serious problem between Jan and Florin: a lack of trust and communication. Somewhere along the line something had gone wrong, and as it had not been addressed, the situation had deteriorated. I now found myself as piggy-in-the-middle. Florin told me things and then Jan told me things. I decided to bide my time. I felt sure that God would provide the right moment for me to play a part in this little soap opera. In the meantime, good progress was being made on site.

Jan was now living in Casa Mea, having given up her flat for financial reasons. This lady gave up a law practice in Texas to devote her time to helping the orphans of Romania. As usual I tried to find out as much as I could about all that went on in the places that I worked in, and I wanted to know more about the little girl Julia. The background to these children was always sketchy and left many questions unanswered, but I was told that Julia's mother was in a mental institution, and it was thought (but not proven) that she was abused by one of the staff.

Anyway, along came little Julia. Julia's grandparents assumed that because their daughter was a mental retard, the grandchild would be also. So from the onset they decided they would not accept the child or have anything to do with her, the result being that Julia and her grandparents had never even seen each other.

That being the case, the authorities took Julia away from her mother and placed her in one of the dreadful state orphanages. Somehow Jan found out about this and successfully applied to adopt Julia. She took her out of the institute and cared for her in Casa Mea. Thankfully, Julia was born perfectly normal and a joy to be with. She captured my heart, and I spent a lot of time with her.

On Saturday it was decided that we would have the day off and go exploring. There was an Englishman who had set up a business out there. His name is Colin Shaw, and he did tailor-made tours of Romania. So, come 10 am we all piled into his Land Rover and set off on a day's tour of the local area. Colin had obviously done his homework, because he knew an enormous amount of Romanian history. He knew all the back roads, the mountain passes, the castles, places like Risnov citadel, and the infamous Bran castle.

We had lunch in a beautiful hotel at the very top of a mountain, with panoramic views all around. We visited an enclosure where two wild wolves were kept. These wolves really were wild but, because of their situation, were somewhat dependent on man for their food. Colin and two others were the only people who were allowed to feed them. Even when being fed they were quite vicious, the female being dominant. They were fed on dead horseflesh and the smell was terrible. That proved to be a good day out. Romania is a beautiful country and it would have been a shame not to do a little bit of exploring.

One of the jobs I decided to do was to lay a concrete path across the front of the property. We had the aggregate and cement on site, so Mihai, Chris, Richard and I made an early start. With no ready-mix plant nearby and no mixer, it all had to be done by hand. I prepared the ground and shuttering, whilst the others did the mixing and barrowing. It was non-stop from early morning until late afternoon - then a good clean up.

I said to the team that that was a good day's work.

Richard's reply was, "Bryan, I thought that it was a good day's work at ten o'clock." Then he promptly collapsed into the wheelbarrow, shattered.

Another time, I used one of the locals to hang a door. He didn't do a very good job and explained to Jan that it was because he felt nervous with me around. Jan just smiled and said not to worry, as everyone is nervous when I was around. I still don't know whether to be pleased or not.

So for the next few weeks this was the pattern of our time in Prejmer. A great deal of work had been done - actually more than I expected. Floors had been laid, ceilings up, bathrooms fitted and tiled (but not finished), rooms created, stairs in, and most of the decorating done. The one big job that was left was the new roof, and I felt that that it was not a job for volunteers and I would give that some detailed thought later.

Being so busy meant that time just flew by, and soon our time here was almost over. Finally it was time to start getting things together for the departure, and make for home. It was the last day for the team; the next day they'd leave for home, and so, to finish things off properly, we decided to have a meal out together. It was a good way of using up whatever Romanian money each had left. Lei cannot be used anywhere but in Romania. Goodbye's said, emails and telephone numbers exchanged, we all promised to meet again. We then went our separate ways. They were a good group and I enjoyed their company.

Sylvia and I stayed on a little longer. Sunday arrived and Florin, along with his brother and their wives, took Sylvia and I up the mountain for a barbecue. This was about an hour's drive away, travelling through many villages, uphill and down dale, with many a sight to see; plus it was a nice warm sunny day. Once there it was a matter of collecting wood for the fire (no charcoal there) and Florin taking charge of the cooking, while some of us went exploring. I was taken to a clearing in the woods. In the centre of this clearing was a 45-gallon drum. This drum was full of dead horsemeat, and it had been left there for some time, to enable it to putrefy. The smell was dreadful, which was how it was intended to be. The smell attracted the wild pigs and boars.

About fifty metres away there was a tree house in which hunters hid themselves, and when these animals came for their feed of horsemeat, the shooting began. This was not my kind of scene so I was glad to get back to the barbecue and a nice feed. It was noticeable that up in the mountains during late afternoon the temperature dropped quite quickly, and Sylvia started to feel the cold. I think that she spoke for everyone, because all seemed happy to start packing up and head for home.

As stated, this was a mountain area and a place where people took their livestock to graze: goats, sheep, cows etc. Shepherds were employed to live in the mountains and care for the animals. On the way back I met one of the shepherds. He was a small man, about five feet tall and dressed for a life in the mountains: woolly hat, thick fleece, and fur-lined boots. He carried a long axe. This was needed because of its many uses: wood chopping, repairing things like fences or the many scattered cabins and huts that he lived in, also as a defence of himself and his charges, i.e. the livestock. More that 30% of the European brown bears live in Romania accompanied by a high proportion of lynx and wolves. Being a shepherd in that country was both a dangerous and hard life.

Before leaving, Jan asked me to put together a program of works (jobs that needed to be done) and in chronological order so that things didn't get done twice. I did this, also giving her a good idea of the costing. I also spoke with Florin about the program, and he assured me that he could handle it all.

With the team already on their way home, it was time for Sylvia and I to do the same; so a good night's sleep, up at 6.30, showered and shaved, breakfast and on the road by 7.30. The aim was to get to Valea Crisului, which was on the other side of Romania and a full day's drive, there to call in on some friends from one of our previous enterprises.

I've said before that Romania is a beautiful country and the road between Brasov and Valea Crisului confirmed this. It led us through some magnificent countryside, over snow-capped mountain passes, valleys and gorges, with many a hairpin bend and lots of villages. This was Transylvania country, Dracula, Bran Castle and the like. It is hard to relate what we were seeing to what Hollywood had led us to believe. Dracula to Romania is what the Loch Ness monster is to Scotland. The story goes that Ceaucescu was aware that he could make money out of scenic sites in the country. He searched the country for a likely looking castle, found one, named it Bran Castle, Dracula's home in the movies, and so created his own little goldmine. A whole industry had sprung up around this castle, and tourists flock there in the thousands. There were hotels, guest houses, shops, stalls, guided walks, and talks, both inside and outside the castle - all at a price of course. We ourselves spent some time there, and it helped make up an interesting day.

Late afternoon and the valley loomed into sight. Soon we were among friends. They didn't know that we were coming but we felt sure that they would give us a great welcome and a bed for the night. Our assumptions were well-founded, as we enjoyed an enthusiastic welcome by all with much celebration. Filimon, the father figure, went out as usual and bought a few beers. In addition to that, he actually killed a pig to celebrate (talk about the prodigal son); we were truly honoured. I must say that these people had no qualms about this sort of behaviour. Butchering their own livestock is simply a way of life for them! In this case, the killing of a pig meant they tied its legs together, felt for the hollow in the neck below the jaw, and using a sledge hammer to drive a long spike down the hollow until it pierced the heart. Then the pig was hauled up by its back legs, cut by its throat and left to bleed. That done and it was lifted into a wheelbarrow and taken to another part of the yard where they had a gas bottle and a burner with a three inch nozzle on the end. This they used to burn off all the hard skin and hairs. From start to finish this was a pretty gruesome business but just everyday life in rural Romania.

These people were really friendly and made a big fuss over Sylvia and I. They insisted that we stay overnight and spend some time with them. Then we could carry on with our journey. This we agreed to do, which meant that everyone was happy. It was there that some encouraging news awaited us. Cristi, the son of the family, who was now 21 years old, was more than halfway through passing his exams to go into the ministry. This was the same young man who we had given some money to many years ago. This was to enable him to go on to further education, having finished his secondary schooling. This told me that it was a wise investment that had been made. Without that further education, who knows where this young man would have finished up. Now he had a good and fruitful life ahead of him.

Praise the Lord!

Wednesday, and it was up early and on the road, another 1,600 miles to travel. We wanted to be home by Saturday. This was a journey that we had done many times, so we knew where all the best stops were and were able to pace ourselves accordingly. Once again we got stopped by the police. The police car pulled in front of us, then a sign lit up saying "Follow me" and we were led into a lay-by.

It was there that we were invited to step out of the vehicle whilst the customs people did a spot check, looking for guns, drugs, cigarettes, or drink. With none of these things in our possession and all our papers in order, we were allowed to carry on with our journey. I told Sylvia that it was the number plate that did it, this being the third time that we had been stopped and always in the same place. Mile after mile we went. The day was warm and sunny, and we needed plenty of stops to take in liquid. We always started looking for our night's lodging around 6pm. That meant that by 7.00 to 7.30 we would have found a place. We had a quiet half hour, then a shower and off to the adjacent restaurant for a nice meal. We were in bed by about 10 o'clock, had a good night's sleep, followed by breakfast at about 8am, and off again on our journey.

This was our procedure until we reached dear old Penryn where we found everything to our satisfaction - another successful leg of our journey with the Lord completed!

Whilst working in Casa Mea, I could see a familiar pattern emerging, a pattern which reminded me of my last project in Dezna, and this was not good news. So, after careful thought, I decided to sit down and write a letter to the trustees of Casa Mea. These trustees were based in Texas, U.S.A., and as such I had never met them.

To the Casa Mea Trustees.
From Bryan
22.09.06.

I have a sneaky feeling that you may know who Bryan is; I'm the guy from England who has been helping out with the work at Casa Mea in Prejmer.

Now that I have spent some time in Prejmer, and learnt a lot more about the current proceedings I feel it right to give you my assessment of the situation, and my feelings and concerns for Casa Mea.

Having spent the last 15 years working in Romania, doing exactly this kind of work, (the renovation of buildings) I can see history repeating itself here, and that's not good news. There are several issues I will comment on, and all based on past experience.

Point one, the folks back home, i.e. you the trustees. It's been my experience that when a project like Casa Mea first takes off, everyone is fired up, full of enthusiasm and running on adrenalin, lots of meetings with folk coming up with lots of ideas and suggestions, but because you don't actually have a hands on experience, dealing with the practicalities on site, the enthusiasm wanes a little and a little apathy sets in, leaving others to get on with it, and being satisfied with the reports from the Front and, letting things just evolve.

I have seen this happen before and believe it to be a perfectly natural development, a human frailty if you like. Not knowing much about Casa Mea or how you operate, I do wonder if you have any idea of the size of this project and the costs involved; most people who get involved in this kind of work don't. They then get somewhat disillusioned after a while because of the costs, and the longevity of the work. My last project being typical, many thousands of pounds spent, and many years in the making.

After having a brief chat with Jan, coupled with my own assessment and observations I can see Casa Mea going the same way. And that's not good news.

Point two. If one looks at the big picture, and wanting Casa Mea to realize its fullest potential, and to get the place up and running as soon as possible, its my opinion that there needs to be a change of attitude, plus you need to be contemplating spending something between 50 and 75,000 dollars minimum. I make reference to Casa Mea and its fullest potential. Let me develop that.

It's my opinion that in Casa Mea you have an ideal situation: a large plot of land, which is ripe for development, more like a ranch. What an opportunity this gives you for self sufficiency, all your root crops, veg and such, potatoes, fruit trees, animal feed, a place to run chickens, pigs, one or two cows. With the chickens you get your eggs, pigs give pork, cows give you milk, this gives yoghurt, cheese, butter and so on and on. Naturally to achieve this means a capital outlay and someone to do the work. You have such a man as a neighbour, Mihai. Each time that I go to Casa Mea to work, I ask for this man to work with me. He is reliable and in my opinion trustworthy, (a rarity in Romania), Mihai could do all this work, and long term the produce will offset the capital outlay. In addition to all that; any excess produce could be sold to the locals at market. This is not pie in the sky stuff, it's actually going on all over rural Romania, so why not Casa Mea?

You have bought this land; you should use it to its fullest potential, and I see no reason why it shouldn't be started now in readiness for a crop next season. It's my experience that forward planning is crucial in Romania

With regards to the building itself - what an opportunity this presents for potential income. I have just returned from Prejmer, having completed the refurbishment of the first floor bedrooms, four in number, each large enough to accommodate at least four children. Jan tells me that you have decided that twelve children will be your target which leaves one large room for a play area.

This means that to function as a home for twelve or more children you don't need the use of the top floor. You have two enormous spaces to turn into accommodation. Two self-contained apartments, used as holiday lets would give a tremendous income, and help with the running cost of Casa Mea. Surely this must be worth considering.

Point three: Volunteers. When one talks about volunteers it always looks good on paper, but the reality is a different matter. There are several kinds of volunteers, most of whom have never done this kind of work before, therefore have no idea what lies ahead of them, work-wise or culture-wise. Again speaking from experience I would suggest that you are not doing yourselves any favours operating this way. In reality what it produces is a stop-start, stop-start mode of operation which only results in dragging the work out, and pushes the completion date further and further away, the exact opposite of what you want.

All volunteers come out with enthusiasm, which is good, but with no building skills, which is not so good. There is work already gone on in Casa Mea, which will need some attention. Not good, we don't want to be doing one job twice. Some volunteers are just a pain in the****. They just come out for a cheap holiday. Ask Jan to tell you about Keith, he was neither use nor ornament. With Keith, duration of stay one week - work output one hour. All this causes frustration and annoyance and in my opinion should be avoided if possible. Question: How does one do that? Well one way is to ask volunteers what building skills they have. If they don't have any then what's the point. If they still want to come just for the experience let them. There is good bunkhouse accommodation at Casa Mea, but charge them 10/15 dollars a night, that way they can enjoy the experience, and it's another source of income for Casa Mea. Casa Mea should be considered a business and run as such. If the volunteers put in an eight hour day five days a week that qualifies them for free board and lodging.

The volunteer and the apartment accommodation is quite separate from where Jan and the children are living, so none of this would impinge on their privacy. Another sore point with me regarding the volunteers is the miss-use of tools. Tools go missing, tools are left out to go rusty, paint brushes gone hard, buckets with plaster left in and gone hard, all these things have to be replaced, which costs money, and time travelling to town to get the replacement, but with proper care and some discipline this need not be necessary. Time is of the essence out there, and it cannot be wasted. Whilst out there I have built up quite a nice tool bank; it now needs to be looked after. It's frustrating and annoying to be willing to give time and money to something, then find you just can't get on with the job because of the lack of tools, nevertheless it is getting better, simply because whilst I am out there I make it compulsory that when tools are used, they are cleaned and put back in there proper place.

Yet another point I must raise. Relying on volunteers, you automatically frustrate the progress, because it inevitably leads to a stop-start situation. Between my spring visit and my autumn visit I could see no evidence of work being done by other volunteers. This is despite the fact there is still lots of work to be done for all trades. If the current practice continues I believe it will be another three or four years before Casa Mea could even consider an opening date. If the volunteers had the much-needed skills it would be different, but in general they don't. Enthusiasm alone won't get the job done. Jan tells me that the lack of funds is a major part of the problem. If so, enter the trustees, and we go back to the beginning of this letter, you need to get fired up once more and start fund raising. This kind of work is a 24 hours a day, 7 days a week effort, and you can't afford to relax.

Relying on volunteers too much will not actually save you money, it will cost you. Again I feel that I must remind you, this is the voice of experience talking to you, and I see history repeating itself here. Again on volunteers, Jan tells me that it is hoped that volunteers will be coming out to help look after the children. Two points on that idea. First I doubt if the authorities would allow it. On one of my other projects the authorities insisted on local carers being employed, with a proper wage structure, annual holidays, one day a week off, with insurance and pension funds provided, all with the proper back up to facilitate this. The second point is: If you had volunteers, one presumes that they would be English-speaking. Now you have the situation whereby the children start their lives learning a foreign language. Surely this would put them at a disadvantage when they start school, having to start learning their own language, thus being behind in class.

A lot of thought needs to be given to this idea of volunteers, and volunteers in general. You may think all this odd coming from a volunteer, but the difference is that I have spent 45 years in the building trade, and the folk that come out whilst I am there do exactly as I say, thus, things get done properly and in chronological order, and doing things that way makes a big difference. Please don't think that I am being too hard on volunteers, but like I said, enthusiasm alone will not get the job done.

One other thing I think you ought to consider - a site manager, someone who knows and understands the building trade. If this were to happen a lot of time and money would be saved, and be a big help to Jan. Jan Calos does not understand the building trade and is not coping. She has her hands full, currently looking after two small children, one of whom has a set of lungs that would stop a train. That in turn means that Jan is not getting the rest that she needs, trying to juggle her mind coping with the children, the foundation, the bureaucrats, and the building. It's all proving too much. She gets extremely frustrated, irritable, and crabby, and if things don't change I can see problems ahead. Her heart is with the children, and I believe that some effort should be made to relieve her of the building responsibility and the fund-raising, thus taking away a lot of the pressure that she is under. If for whatever reason this lady cracks up you will be in a lot of trouble. Jan may deny some of this, but others and I actually see it.

A site manager would help enormously. In addition to helping Jan it would speed up the work, and probably save money, and bring the opening date nearer.

I also think that it would be helpful if an approach were made to the local authorities to ask what would be the minimum amount of work completed to allow Casa Mea to open. This would give you a target to aim for. I suggest this because on my last project we did this, only to be told that the whole project had to be completed before an occupation permit would be granted, even though some of the rooms weren't going to be used by the children. Either way you would know exactly where you stood and could set out your stall accordingly. Keeping on with the authorities, it's anticipated that next year Romania will be in the European Union. That being you may have to cope with a whole new set of added rules and regulations. A minimum wage to start with, currently in the U.K is about £6 per hour. This would add considerably to your weekly running costs.

But a big one for your consideration would be child-safety. Currently in Casa Mea you have no provision for fire protection: no smoke alarms, no sprinkler systems, no fire-check doors. These are big issues, and I urge you to consider them, even if the authorities don't insist I believe that you should consider it. We are talking small babies here. They can't get up and run - food for thought at least. Again I want to remind you that you have taken on an enormous enterprise here, and have already passed the point of no return, and these things have to be faced up to. The Romanian authorities don't take any prisoners.

Up to now all I have written about is the development of the building and grounds. Have you considered the running costs? Again from experience I can tell you such an enterprise doesn't come cheap: the weekly/monthly/annual running costs are unending, and are obligatory. This is why I suggest that Casa Mea itself should try to be self sufficient in produce, and use its facilities to generate income. You are going to need all the help you can get.

One way of getting such help is to approach the local child-welfare office. We did this with the first project that I was involved in; the agency paid us a visit and was delighted with what we had done. An agreement was reached. We allowed them to place their children in our home. They then accepted the responsibility for staffing the home, paying all wages and food allowance etc, we retain ownership of property and are responsible for the maintenance costs. Both parties were delighted. The place is full of children, and we were released from a lot of financial pressure - just something else for you to think about.

So to summarise - with a big successful effort in fund raising, you could do away with the use of volunteers and use local labour, working under a site manager, bringing the project back to life, thus speeding up the opening date of Casa Mea, and safeguarding Jan. Developing the land and the top floor would be a great help towards your financial responsibility. If the finances are in place I see no reason why Casa Mea shouldn't be up and running by the end of 2007. If this is not the case, then you need to sit down and ask why. Forward planning and continuity is what you should aim for.

It's important to me that you understand my motive for writing this letter. The reason we are all involved in this work is the children, and I don't want to see Casa Mea get bogged down (and its heading that way) like other projects, so this letter is being written with encouragement in mind and nothing else.

I wish you all well.

That done, I just sat back and awaited results. Three weeks later I got an email, stating that as a result of my letter all work had been suspended until further notice. Advice was being taken, and in January there was to be a full meeting with all concerned and decisions made, and I would be informed of that decision. I felt happy with that. At least I had woken them up as to the realities of the situation and I felt that any change would be an improvement.

In January I got my answer from the Casa Mea trustees. It seemed that they had taken notice of some of my comments in the letter and asked if I would take part in a three-way telephone conversation with two of the trustees in Texas. I agreed, so at a given time on a given day, this conversation took place, and it proved to be highly beneficial to all concerned.

They had decided to employ a site manager to oversee the works. Not only that - they actually offered me the job. Being an employee, I would naturally have a salary. I declined the offer, stating that I didn't do this work for financial gain. They understood where I was coming from, and so we moved on. But the good news was that they had apparently raised sufficient funds to employ local professional builders to do the work, thus eliminating the dependence on volunteers. That had to be good news for all concerned, especially Jan.

Fund raising played a big part in this work, and rather than go to individuals as I had in the past, I planned to do something different; I was going to organise a concert.

First thing was who to ask to take part. Then things started to fall into place when a fellowship member told me that he had just joined a local men's choir. Then my brain went into overdrive. I got the phone numbers of the musical director and secretary and things started to happen. The answer to my proposal for a concert was a firm *"Yes!"* Not only that but I was told that there was a ladies' choir based in Torpoint that would also like to be involved. I also approached a gifted singer in our fellowship and she agreed to do a solo performance. So one week after I had the idea, it all seemed to fall into place.

I put the musical directors of both choirs in touch with each other, and together with Lee our soloist they all worked out a three-hour program. Because the ladies had to travel from the Plymouth area they asked if some refreshments could be made available ("a cup of tea and a few scones would be nice"), and Sylvia agreed to take charge of these things for me.

The men's choir charged £90 to cover certain expenses, all of which was acceptable. Flyers were printed, both by Emmanuel and myself and spread around the town and other churches. Now I just prayed for a full house and hoped that everyone would have an enjoyable evening. Come the night of the performance, and with John Hills presiding as compère, everything went well. A good number of people turned up, and the money raised made a tremendous difference to the next project.

THAT WHICH BINDS US TOGETHER

SHOULD BE STRONGER THAN

THAT WHICH PULLS US APART

KRIZBAV

God was obviously still at work!

The good news that came my way that week came from one of the team that I worked with on Casa Mea. He invited me to join him on another building project in the Brasov area. This invitation I gladly embraced.

I was particularly happy about this, because it was in the Brasov area that I would be able to return to Casa Mea and see Julia and Jan, also Florin and his family. All these people were very special to me because of the circumstances that brought us all together. I also believed that all was part of God's bigger plan. The money raised from the Choir concert could be put to good use. The new team was made up of five women and six men, only two of whom I knew, having worked with them before. The rest were strangers to me.

I like to know as much as I can about a situation before starting off, so I got in touch with David, the guy who was organising the trip, and asked one or two questions. First of all: it would be nice to know exactly where the new project was. I was informed that it was a place called Krizbav, about ten miles east of Brasov. The second and most important question was: what building skills did the team have?

The answer was: none.

To me this did not necessarily mean bad news. I was told that the bulk of the work to be done was plaster boarding, electrics and plumbing. With the studwork already in place it shouldn't prove to be too difficult to teach others how and what to do to get the job done. Anyway this was just one more challenge to overcome and glorify God in the process.

With the team virtually established (it was early days and experience had taught me that many things could happen), responsibilities were allocated to various people: who was to take charge of the food, what tools were needed, finance and transport. The way things turned out, all the right decisions were made and the whole operation went quite smoothly. I myself was not involved at this stage, the reason being that all of them lived quite close to one another in the Stratford area, which enabled them to meet up and discuss things. That said, I was kept informed by email and kept fully up to date with the goings on. I was able to have some input in matters with regard to the building work.

With the flights booked, it was just a matter of waiting for the departure time to arrive. We flew from Luton airport to Bucharest-Opteni airport. Departure time, from Luton, was 11.05am with check in time two hours before that. All things considered I thought it best to travel from Penryn to Stratford-upon-Avon the day before, spend a night with Richard (one of the team members) then make a one and a half hour's journey from Stratford to Luton on the morning of the flight. That way I would be fresh, and there would be no need to rush. That was the plan. Sadly it didn't turn out that way.

I arrived at Richard's place about mid-afternoon feeling quite good and relaxed. As I had never been to Stratford before, Richard and his daughter took me for a walk. This was Shakespeare country, also a hot spot for tourists, which was made obvious by the many different nationalities wandering around. After a McDonalds, we went home. The girl went to bed and Richard prepared a meal for us both.

Richard and his wife had parted. They shared the daughter between them, a sad situation but quite civilised.

I had driven nearly three hundred miles that day, so it wasn't long before I decided to retire. I knew what was ahead of me and I wanted to stay as fresh as possible. Up at 7am, I showered and got myself ready to travel.

Another team member joined us that morning. This was Jan, and she was travelling from the Shrewsbury area. Jan arrived about 9.30. We loaded all our cases into Richard's car and set off on the one and a half hour drive to the airport. Driving along, suddenly Richard used his mobile phone to call a friend, telling him that we were on our way to the airport and that as we were well ahead of schedule we would call in and have a cup of tea and a bacon sandwich. This we did, and Richard sat there talking. Jan and I had no idea how far it was to the airport from where we were, so we just politely sat there.

Time rolled on and this was pointed out to Richard who, when realising the time, started to panic a little. We piled into his car and set off once more. Then disaster struck. We hit the motorway and the traffic was bumper-to-bumper and not moving. Not having much option, Richard said he would have to take a chance and use the hard shoulder. This was a stressful time for us all. Our departure time was getting very close.

At last we arrived at the airport. It was decided that Jan and I should be dropped off at the terminal entrance, taking the luggage with us, and go and check in. Richard now had to go and park the car. When Jan and I arrived at the desk we are told that we had two minutes to be processed, then the gate closed. As soon as we were in possession of our boarding pass, we cleared security. Thankfully the plane was running a little late, so now we were able to relax a little. Sadly this was not the case for Richard. He arrived about five minutes after the gate closed and there was no way that they were going to let him in. So Richard missed the plane and all for a bacon sandwich. Of all the people who could miss the plane, Richard would be the last one to choose. He had been out to Romania before. I had worked with him, and he was familiar with the work that we were going to do. He would be sorely missed.

One of the things that happened in planning this trip was to buy some T-shirts and have a logo printed across the chest. The logo said "Upon this Rock." So, wearing these T-shirts we were able to recognise other team members. As we were strangers to one another, this proved to be a wise decision as each one was recognisable. Soon we were all together and started to get to know each other.

I thought to myself that this was going to be an interesting mission. One chap worked in a solicitor's office, one was an actor, one a writer, one a salesman, another in computers and the rest housewives. Apart from Damien none had any building experience, and six of them had never been to Romania before. I just thought to myself: one more challenge to overcome.

We were told the flight time to Bucharest was two hours and forty minutes, so as we took off at midday, we would be there by 3pm - an hour to clear the airport, then a four-hour drive to Krizbav, plus we needed to eat. So I prepared myself for a late night. The team, although novices, proved to be good pupils. Not only were they willing to learn but also to show great enthusiasm. There was a good combination of qualities. I only had to tell and show them once. They then grabbed a hammer and saw, and away they went. The sleeping arrangements were such that we each had our privacy, although sleeping on a thin mattress on the floor left something to be desired.

We split into three teams, chose a room each, and then started to plasterboard the ceilings. Throughout the day there was a chorus of 'Ooohs' and 'Arrh's as thumbs were hit. Michael actually sawed into his own leg - talk about learning the hard way. Looking for Lindsey, one time, all I had to do was to follow a trail of blood. Thankfully none of the mishaps were serious. I told them that they were not to consider them scars, but medals.

As each day went by, they got better and better, and quicker and quicker. Not only that, the quality of the work was very good. This kind of work was something new to them, as they had done nothing like it before. They had nothing to compare it with, so by way of encouragement I told them that they were doing very well and should feel very pleased with themselves. That kind of encouragement worked well because their confidence grew and the cries of "Bryan, help!" grew less as the time went on.

To help with the local economy we employed some local labour, young men from nearby. A lot of the materials had to be carried upstairs and this was where they proved to be a great help. I thought there was a limit as to what we could ask the ladies to do, no matter how willing they were. Plus, the locals were taught some construction skills. The place became a hive of industry, with great changes happening on a daily basis. Florin, the local man who was responsible for this project, just sat back with a big smile on his face.

We had one toilet on site plus a shower facility (mostly it was just cold water), but working in these conditions one was just grateful for anything. With no kitchen facilities, we bought ourselves a kettle and teapot, some bread and cheese for lunch, and survived on that throughout each day, actually using a handsaw as a bread knife - oh the joys of mission work! So come evening time, one by one the team stopped work and got cleaned up. By 7 pm we were all ready for the bumpy ride into Brasov for a hot meal. The drive there took less than one hour, which usually meant that by the time we had parked up and found somewhere to dine, we didn't start to eat until 9 o'clock.

Those evening meals weren't just about eating. With not much time for chitchat on site, it was a good time to get to know one another a little better. Although it wasn't excessively hot, after a day's hard work I was always ready for a cold beer. With a cold beer inside me, good food, and good company, quality time was enjoyed by all. No one usually got to bed before 12.30am.

Normally at home I am in bed by about 10 o'clock, so the late nights quickly took a toll on me; so much so that on the Tuesday I decided not to go to town but to stay behind and have an early night. I wasn't exactly alone; Florin was on site. Although he did not speak English, we got on fine; plus with a small boiler on site, he rustled me up some hot water, which was fantastic. I lay in a hot bath for about an hour. By 9pm I was in bed, and by 9.05 I was asleep.

Come the Wednesday night and some other members of the team were flagging. Apparently they too were not used to the late nights either. A 'pow-wow' was called for and it was decided that the following day we would all remain at home. Damien called on one of his friends, who brought out a case of beer and several pizzas. We had a game of Charades, a few stories were told, then one by one we all drifted off to our rooms and had an earlier night than usual. It was agreed that everyone benefitted from that, and it showed in the renewed vigour that was apparent the next day. The work was repetitive, and by now all were quite good at what they were doing, so the output was steady. Florin was continually impressed.

Soon the day of departure was almost upon us. As the next day was our last day, it was a case of winding down and making sure that we finished whatever job we were involved in. We didn't want to leave a room partly done, so to that end we helped each other out. We then started to get packed up, showered, minibus loaded, and ready for the four hour drive to Bucharest airport, before making our way to the Youth Hostel, where we were going to spend our last night.

On the way to Bucharest we planned to visit an orphanage way up in the mountains. This proved to be different from the usual Romanian orphanages as it was in a monastery and run by nuns, who were charming people: courteous, considerate, and showing a great deal of affection towards the children. The children were well-clothed and well-fed. They were bonny and happy; above all they were loved. It was a joy to be with them, a good feeling to take home with me.

Praise the Lord!

I had money given to me by a member of Emmanuel Church and I felt that this would be the right place to use it, so I passed it on to the nun who had been looking after us. After that, we left and made our way to Bucharest and the youth hostel. It was late now: 9.30 or 10pm. No-one seemed bothered about eating, so after ordering our taxis for 6am, it was off to bed. With limited washing facilities, it was up at 5am to get in the queue. That done, we went downstairs and into the waiting taxis, then off to the airport. Once there, we had time for some breakfast and boarded the plane. Two hours later we were in Luton, said our 'goodbye's and, after promising to meet again, went our separate ways.

Jan and I met up with Richard who had come to meet us. He drove us back to his place where we picked up our respective vehicles. Jan then made her way to Shrewsbury, and I headed for Cornwall. At about 10.30 that night I was home, safe and well. Another giant step had been made to help improve the lot of some of the world's most unfortunate children. I was tired but I felt good.

For the following three years, I said it would be my last trip, but somehow the work wouldn't let go of me. Each year that I went out to Romania I either took a new team with me, or got an invitation to join a team - often a team of enthusiastic volunteers but with none of the necessary skills needed to make things happen. So at the parting of the ways each year I have been greeted with a chorus of cries, "Bryan you must come again next time!" and, "We need you!" and, "Who is going to show us what to do?" I have to confess that already having a heart for this kind of work, I don't take too much persuading, so with the understanding and support of Sylvia I planned for the coming year's trip with the usual enthusiasm.

The 2008 trip was planned to leave on the 11th May. The good thing was that this time I knew exactly where we were going, what stage the building was at, and exactly what was needed material-wise, tool wise, and skill wise. That was a big plus! When the planning of the trip was in its infancy there were ten people who were on board, but as time rolled by one-by-one some dropped off until, at the time of making our flight arrangements, there were just three remaining. After so many years of doing the work I am never surprised by this. I'm always disappointed, but not surprised. Of the three flying out, I knew David from a previous trip. The other, Tony, was a stranger to me. The good news was that Tony was an experienced builder and that more than made up for any disappointment.

We flew out from Gatwick this time and out flight time was 6.15am. That meant we had to be at the check-in at 4.15. So, all things considered, I again thought it best to travel up to David's place the day before we were due to leave. Spending the night there meant I would get a few hours' sleep before we set off on our journey, David's place being two hours away from Gatwick, as opposed to six hours from Penryn.

We arrived in Gatwick at about 2am, bleary-eyed, but alert. There we met up with Tony and all three of us went for a refreshing cup of coffee and a chat. I had to say that I was encouraged by Tony. He not only was involved in the building trade, he was also self-employed, and it soon became obvious that he talked the same language as me. Being self-employed meant that you had to have the confidence to make decisions and the ability to think ahead. The immediate future looked bright.

Praise the Lord!

The duration of the flight was about two and a half hours and I cat-napped my way through it. There were drinks and food on offer at a price, but I didn't feel like eating at that time of the morning. With our watches being put forward two hours to accommodate local time it meant that it was about 1 am by the time we cleared the airport at Bucharest, followed by a four hour drive in Addi's car to Brasov. So we finally got to our accommodation by about mid-afternoon.

The place was clean and comfortable and we had proper beds. That was very important; a good night's sleep was essential when doing this work. The kitchen facilities were minimal, but that didn't matter as we planned to eat out each night. Nevertheless, the first thing we had to do was to get our breakfast food bought: cereal, tea, coffee, milk, bread etc. Again it was essential that we started the day off properly, and a good breakfast helped do that.

More good news greeted us. We had been joined by two other people, Nigel and Roselyn, a married couple, English but living in Vienna. Nigel was a project manager and was between jobs. So they both travelled by motor-cycle to Brasov and would be with us for the duration of our stay. So with Florin and his son, Gabi, plus Gabi's friend, and with Damien floating in and out, the team grew considerably. With what we were planning to do, that was good news!

The first day on site and a few things were a bit hit and miss, like who did what, what time we needed to be up and about on site and what time we worked until. I decided to take the initiative and stated Rule No.1: We needed to be up by 6.30 in the morning, toiletries done and breakfast over by 7.30, working by 7.35, finishing the day at 6.30pm, with a plentiful supply of tea or coffee throughout the day and a sandwich about 1.00pm. That would keep us going. All agreed, and by the end of our time it proved to be a good strategy, as much was accomplished and all stayed fresh.

The work that we were doing was tiling the bathrooms, plus some remedial work to the electrics. An American team had been over earlier and had run in the electrics, positioning the switches and power points. The problem was they had positioned the points halfway on the plasterboard and halfway on the tiling, resulting in the sockets not being fixed to a flat surface. So, it being easier and quicker to cut the plasterboard rather than the tiles, I decided to do just that and raised all the switches and power points about six inches, the end result being a much better job and speeded up the tiling in the process.

The team worked well together; so much so that we completed all the bathroom walls, plus the washing and drying room, and then made a start on the floors. On the Thursday night Damien organised a barbecue, and Florin, our friend from Prejmer, came and did the cooking for us. It was a task he revelled in and, I might add, he was very good at it. Nothing got burnt, so with the usual chicken legs, sausages, beef burgers and the like, plus a crate of beer to wash it all down, an enjoyable time was had by all.

It was on this trip that I met with Clare, a remarkable young lady. The story was that returning from work one day, she was somewhat accosted on the street by two very young boys, four or five years old, brothers who were homeless beggars struggling to survive.

Even at the young age of nineteen, and single, Clare did not have the heart to just pass them by. She took them to her parents' home where she was living and asked if they could stay and live with the family, promising to take care of them herself. Clare's parents agreed and the boys moved in.

Clare and her parents then started the process of adopting the two youngsters. Their application was successful and now this young, single lady had a ready-made family. All this happened six or seven years before when Clare was only nineteen years of age, but the story didn't end there. Since then Clare had adopted a little girl called Madelyn and now all three children, Elvis, Thomas and Madelyn were no longer homeless or beggars. They were cared for and loved.

I found that an incredible thing for someone so young to do, especially when one thinks of what Clare actually gave up i.e. her last teenage year, her social life and all the other activities young people do. But it was soon obvious that the pleasure she got from these three young children more than made up for her sacrifice.

Romania is an amazing country. I've seen amazing cruelty and callous behaviour from some, and equally, amazing kindness and love from others. I suspect that if I thought about this in some detail, it isn't just applicable to Romania. It's a worldwide thing; there's good and bad everywhere. But for me personally it's people like Clare who give me hope that all is not lost with the human race.

It was Friday now and our last day for actually working on site. Florin was delighted with what had been achieved and using his son, Gabbi, as an interpreter, expressed his gratitude. After coming to Romania for eighteen years I still hadn't been to the capital or seen any of the interesting places there. So as we all particularly wanted to see Ceausescu's palace, we set of for a day's sightseeing.

We travelled by train from Brasov to Bucharest. The trains were clean, fast and punctual with comfortable seats, also with refreshments available and very cheap. A four-hour journey cost about £1 each. It proved to be one very hot day, too hot for walking in fact, so we got a taxi to take us to the palace. It was a magnificent building and very impressive, but the cost in human misery in building it didn't bear thinking about. Soon we had seen enough of Bucharest. To me one city is much like any other, and we also had other things on our mind.

Before we left for Bucharest, we had a visit from Damien who told us that we had an invitation to a celebration party. This was to take place in a small town, not far from where we were. It meant more travelling. We debated about whether or not to go, but not wanting to be guilty of refusing Romanian hospitality, we decided it was okay. This proved to be a good decision as we were made very welcome, and we not only had a sumptuous meal but also a night's accommodation thrown in.

There were about twelve or fourteen people at the party. Everyone sat around a big table, which was laden with food. Once the first course was eaten, another replaced it. This was repeated a third time, and each course was different from the last. We had potatoes first, then meat and chicken and then salad etc. This was followed by dessert, ice cream and fruit, all taken at a leisurely pace, and accompanied by much singing and frivolity.

With English being spoken by two or three of the younger element, we were not left wondering what was going on. I have found that Romanians, in general, are not at all short on hospitality. As time went on, one or two people decided to call it a night, so things were called to a halt. We were now transported to our accommodation. This was the home of a very elderly lady, and it was set in its own grounds - a massive dark wooden structure. In the dark of the night it looked pretty scary.

This lady had a big heart for stray cats and dogs, of which she had many. I think there were eight dogs of various sizes and colour and a dozen cats On meeting these animals for the first time it proved to be a bit daunting, but after a short time things settled down and there was no problems. These animals were well-trained and disciplined.

Once inside this building it was something to behold. The furniture and décor matched the outside: lots of dark wood, ornately carved, curved staircase, shelves with old pots and memorabilia. Inside the front door was a full female national costume: very colourful and attractive. This elderly lady actually still wore this as and when she needed to.

I found this place quite fascinating. By now, it being around midnight, I thought it best to find my room and retire. The others decided to stay up a little longer and share a bottle of wine. That was not for me. I felt that my sleep was more important than small talk. The next morning (Saturday) and, as usual, I was the first one up. I found it hard to lie there awake staring at the ceiling. I would much rather get up and explore this fascinating building.

With no one yet around I wandered from room to room. The kitchen was a wonder to perceive: really old and antiquated, a stone heater, 10cm pipe work exposed around the walls, stone floors, and quite cold. It was like stepping back in time. I wandered outside into the garden where I found that, in addition to the cats and dogs, there were chickens and geese, fruit trees, and a vegetable plot. Although the lady owner was elderly she was very capable and active. I 'took my hat off' to her.

It was not long before others started to stir and faces began to appear. Coffee was brought in and we started to say our goodbyes. Initially we were somewhat reluctant to accept the invitation to the celebration, but I was so glad that we had. Meeting these people, enjoying their company, seeing how they celebrated, this building and its owner, had proved to be a great joy and an eye-opener. Bags packed, we were then driven about half a mile to the bus station. A regular mini bus service then transported us right to the main airport entrance. I am very impressed by the transport system in Romania. I have travelled by train, taxi, bus, and plane, and everything was clean, efficient and punctual. I don't ask for more than that.

Our plane took off on time and arrived in the U.K. on time. After spending some time trying to find David's car, it was off to his home, a cup of tea and a six hour drive to Cornwall. I finally arrived home at about midnight to find Sylvia alive and well. I found that I was still a little 'hyped up', so rather than go straight off to bed I had a bowl of cornflakes and a nice chat with Sylvia. Slowly, as I now started to relax, tiredness started to overcome me. So it was off to bed and a start to my recovery period.

It had been another eventful time on my journey with the Lord. A lot of work was done, moving the project that much nearer to completion. I met lots of new people and I felt that I had learnt much about another culture, and its people.

April 2009 and again my thoughts turned to Romania and the project in Krizbav. Before we left, after our last visit, I had had a conversation with Florin.

He had told me that he had a son who lived in America. After explaining the situation to him, this son had promised to gather a team around him and make the trip to Krizbav; the aim being to complete the work and get the place open and ready for use. Sadly, after some enquiries, I found out that this had not happened. So now that I knew what the situation was, I made contact with David who lived in the Rugby area. After some discussion on what was needed, and not wanting to leave a project unfinished, we decided one more trip would be necessary.

Now history started to repeat itself: the planning, the dates, a team, finance and so on. We were both seasoned campaigners by now, so it was not too long before things started to happen. By mid-July we had nearly everything in place: finance, team, program and dates. I would be taking two men from Emmanuel Church with me: Steve Thomas, and Rhys Moosa, with the added bonus of Steve being a qualified builder. This would be a first for both of these men so, as was my usual practice, I had a lengthy chat with them. With Steve I got the impression that it was just something that he wanted to do, a mixture of curiosity and adventure. Rhys was more specific, stating that he wanted to expand the kingdom of God through this work. Whatever their reasons, I was glad of their willingness to be involved. I felt very sure that it would be of great benefit to both of them. The duration of the trip was to be for two weeks and that should be enough to do what had to be done.

Come 4.30am on Saturday the 23rd of July and Rhys' father picked us up in his car and drove us to Truro Bus station. The bus was on time and we left at 5 o'clock. After a six-hour journey we arrived at Heathrow at 11 o'clock. Our flight departure time was 17:00 hours, which gave us plenty of time to freshen up and have something to eat. That done, we then waited for the arrival of David and Jane. Airports, being very busy places, meant that the place was packed with human traffic, and this was one of the times when I was grateful for a mobile phone. It made contact easy, and soon we were all together.

After checking in and going through security with no problems we again had time to relax. This gave the other team members time to get to know each other. I had always felt that there should be a bonding of the team from the first day, as for two weeks we would be living, working, and sleeping in close proximity of one another, so we needed to be able to do that in the right frame of mind.

I had left it to David to make contact with others who had made the journey in the past, to find out if they would be interested in joining us. One person responded with a 'Yes'. Jan said that she, her partner, two daughters and her sister would also be willing to make the trip. Again that was encouraging as it meant that we would have a complement of ten people on board. Four people (David, Jane, David's wife, Rhys and myself) would be staying for two weeks. Steve would be leaving after one week and Jan and company would be joining us for the second week. I felt at peace about that. The fact that half of the team were women didn't faze me as there was lots of decorating to do, and I felt sure that would be where they would be most useful.

The Lufthansa flight took off on time, and after changing aircraft at Frankfurt and moving our watches forward two hours to accommodate local time, we arrived at Bucharest Opteni at 23.30. There we were picked up by George and his minibus which took us on the final leg of this journey - a three hour drive to Krizbav. It was now 3am on Sunday, and Steve, Rhys and I had been on the road for nigh on 24 hours. Ten minutes after arriving on site, I was in bed.

Despite my tiredness I was still up by 7am, had a cup of tea and wandered around the building. I was quite surprised and impressed by what greeted me - a big change since my last visit. Florin, the man in charge and responsible for this project, who actually lived on site whilst we were there, was also about. This man spoke not a word of English, and I spoke no Romanian. Nevertheless, we were old friends, and necessity being the mother of invention, we did communicate. It seemed that Florin's son, who lived in America and had who promised to arrange for a team to come to Krizbav, hadn't made it, but the good news was that he had sent the money raised

($25.000), courtesy of his fellowship and which Florin had obviously put to good use.

My patrol around the building showed that all the electrics were finished and working. It was the same with the plumbing, with hot and cold running water in each of the bathrooms. Ditto the central heating, and 'praises to the Lord' as there were flush toilets. Out there these were the height of luxury. In addition to this, the kitchen and dining area floors had been tiled, plus the place was reasonably tidy. I was impressed and encouraged.

It had already been agreed that we would not be working on this our first day on site. We needed to get over our journey. I needed to prioritise the workload and allocate the jobs to each individual, plus we needed to go into Brasov and buy our food. It was also agreed that we would eat on site for three days and then go into Brasov and indulge ourselves with a proper meal. In addition to all that, both Steve and Rhys were keen to see the local environment and the inhabitants. So, whilst I did my homework, I let the others sleep in a bit longer.

By 10 o'clock everyone was up and about. I had my list for food needed (which I had prepared back home) and our transport arrived, so off we went into town.

Food bought, and the visit to the builder's merchant over, it was a wander round the Piazza. This place is alive with restaurants and bars. It was a hot and sunny day and the world and his wife were out. This was a special time for Rhys and Steve, as all this was something new to them. With the temperature in the high 90's it was felt by all that a nice cold beer would be most welcome and after that somewhere to eat. By now it was early evening so we made our way back to our home and got ready for our first Monday on site.

Old habits die hard, so again I was up at 6am. First things first, so I had a cup of tea with my quiet time whilst sat on the veranda. This was a special time for me. With no one around I was able to just sit and contemplate. It was there that I found a peace about things.

Kettle back on and brought to the boil, table laid, things were made ready for breakfast. Soon sleepy-eyed bodies began to appear, and by 8.30 work was started.

Steve, being experienced, agreed to take on the wall tiling. I also thought that there might be some benefit to Rhys if he worked with Steve. This would be a learning curve for Rhys and would help to move the work along a bit faster. Rhys agreed and dealt with the cutting of tiles and grouting, thus gaining knowledge and experience, which would be (and was) of benefit later on. As a team they got on fine.

David and Jane got on with the second coat of emulsion on the ceilings, whilst Addi and I clad the ceiling to the outside veranda. Addi, the third son of Florin, spoke English very well. He was an essential part of the team. Without him being present to translate with Florin, life would have been difficult. Jane accepted the responsibility for catering. A regular supply of tea or coffee throughout the day helped to keep spirits high. We had lunch about noon and wound the day up at about 6pm. Dinner over by 8 o'clock, dishes washed, then it was a cold beer and a game of cards. I was usually in bed by 10 o'clock. This was a pattern of our working days.

Because the food on offer from the local shop was quite limited, it was agreed that we would go out for a meal every third day. On the second day (Tuesday) of our eating in, David prepared the evening meal - a meat dish, a kind of stew. The ingredients were bought from the local shop, and no one was able to identify the meat. That evening and the following day most of us suffered an upset tummy, but none more so than Steve who felt really poorly. That day Steve spent most of the day in distress and just generally took things easy.

The following day (Wednesday) we went into town to eat. The team, other than Steve, were now over our discomfort, and tucked into our meal. Steve sat with us but couldn't face another meal. It was now that I started to show some concern. Steve had gone grey in colour, started to shake, convulse, and vomit. He wasn't communicating, so Addi was told to call for an ambulance. Within five or six minutes the medics were on the scene, took one look at Steve, and he was on the way to hospital. We followed in our bus, had a time of prayer about the whole situation, and when we were assured that he would be all right, we left for Krizbav. Steve was kept in overnight, pumped out, and released the following afternoon. Apparently it was some kind of food poisoning.

After some discussion about this incident, it was agreed that we would not eat anything that we didn't recognise, and that we would stick to eggs, chicken, bread and potatoes etc. With Steve now fully recovered, the team was back to full strength and steady progress was made.

Before I had left home I was given about twenty or so high quality teddy bears. These bears, about eight inches high, and of every bright colour imaginable, proved to be a great introduction to the local community, being within walking distance from where we were working. As I could actually see and hear children playing I thought that now would be a good time to pay them a visit and start my distribution. Some mums and dads were present and made no objection to my presence, and the children were enthralled. Their smiles were worth something that money can't buy. It's amazing; something that someone had no use for now brought great joy into so many young lives.

A few weeks before I left home Soani got in touch with me. During our chat I told him of my intended visit to Krizbav. I had known Soani for eighteen years. He was one of the first three children that we got out of a Romanian hellhole, the others being Tommi and Maria. Soani said that he would dearly love to make the trip from Oradia and join me for a long weekend.

Soani has an infectious character and was an absolute joy to be with, a strong Christian and highly principled. He arrived on the Saturday morning and stayed until the Wednesday night. Our meeting was quite emotional. He dropped his case several metres away and just ran to me, hugging me and saying, "Bryan, Bryan!" I was genuinely moved.

During Soani's stay with us, he phoned Maria, telling her of my presence in Brasov. She insisted that we spoke to each other. Of course I was delighted. Maria was positively bubbling with excitement, telling me how happy she was and that she was actually working with handicapped children. Maria then said something that really meant a lot to me. She said, "Thank you Bryan, for giving me a good start in life." That alone meant that all I had been through over the past eighteen years had been worthwhile. Whilst Soani was with us, he worked jolly hard. Come the Wednesday evening and I escorted him to his train. That was quality time.

Praise the Lord!

Prior to Soani's arrival we lost Steve. Steve had only ever intended to stay for the first week as he had a prior family commitment. The day after Soani's arrival (Saturday) Jan and the others arrived. So for the second week we were ten in number.

One day as I was working on the rear veranda, a young lady with a little girl came walking across the field. She was carrying a plastic container, which she promptly filled with water from our outside tap. A short conversation between the lady and Florin took place, and I detected a little tension between them. I asked Florin if there was a problem.

He explained that these two, the lady and the little girl, were gypsies, that they lived nearby and that their home had no running water; hence this journey, which happened several times a day. There is little love lost between the Romanians and the gypsies, hence the tension that I felt. I have stated elsewhere in this journal that the gypsy people are the poorest of the poor in this country. And these two epitomised that fact.

Inside where we were working, we had a large bin full of bonbons (sweets) so each day I made sure that I was on hand to give this little girl a handful. Being so poor, sweets were a luxury item to these people, and that was made obvious by the look on the little girl's face. After a few days, they looked forward to coming over, and I looked forward to seeing them.

The lady could speak no English, so communication was limited. But I did learn that her name was Ramona, her husband was named Sorbin and the little girl's name was Elainer. One day, I also learnt that the following day was the little girl's third birthday. As we had already planned to go into town the following day, I decided to do a little private shopping. I bought a few goodies, a number three badge, a cake and a bottle of lemonade. That evening I was a privileged guest at a very special party. Elainer actually quivered with excitement. It never ceases to amaze me what a little unconditional love can do.

Jobwise, things were going very well. David, being in charge of finance, kept us informed with regard to that situation and so all the necessary materials were always on hand. Mostly the ladies got on with the painting, whilst the men did the heavier work. Rhys learned a lot and was using muscles he never knew he had. On one occasion, when Rhys and I were sitting alone, I asked him what all this had meant to him. One of the things, he replied, was how dissatisfied he had become with his mundane life in Falmouth. And with opportunities like Krizbav around, there were much more interesting and challenging things to life. I was impressed with his answer.

On Friday, our penultimate day, we started to wind things down. We had to leave at 8am the next day. Our flight left at 13.00 hours. We had to check in two hours before flight time and it was a three-hour drive to the airport, so all our packing had to be done that night. Both Jane and I had some local currency left so we decided to pool it. Then Florin and I went to the local shop to spend it. This resulted in two large carrier bags full of groceries, which I took to Ramona. Ramona and Sorbin showed their gratitude with a hug and, as I left, I caught a little glistening in Ramona's eyes. Words were not needed.

That night the team went into Brasov for one final meal. Both Rhys and I decided to give it a miss, have a bath, something to eat, then sit on the veranda and watch the sun go down on our last night in Krizbav. The following morning our 'goodbye's were said to Florin and company. Florin, in turn, spoke of his appreciation for all that had been done. Transport arrived on time and we arrived at Bucharest airport on time. As two teams had arrived at different times and were departing on different flights, it was here that we said our 'goodbye's.

Our plane left on time and after changing flights at Dusseldorf we finally arrived and cleared Heathrow at 18.00 hours. Rhys and I said 'cheerio' to David and Jane, and then had to wait until 23.40 for the arrival of our bus, which took us on the final leg of our journey to Truro.

I walked through my front door at 8.05pm, and was greeted by a smiling Sylvia. Two eventful weeks, lives touched, attitudes changed, lessons learned, new friendships formed, blessings shared and God was glorified. It doesn't get much better than that. But, once again it did leave the big question:

Where do I go from here?

For the past few years I had been asking the good Lord if it was time for me to hang up my suitcase. The fact that I hadn't yet done that clearly indicated that the answer was "No." But at the near completion of each project I still asked the same question.

Both Sylvia and I were at an age where we needed to pace ourselves and I didn't like to leave her alone for any length of time. I had never wanted to leave a job half done, and with Krizbav almost completed, I again asked the question, "Is this the time for me to bow out, and pass the baton on to a younger person?"

My heart said "No," but my head said, "Yes." Since I started this work twenty years ago, I have had to learn to trust God and I have to constantly remind myself of that.

As I write this, and having not long returned from Romania, I do have plenty of time to dwell on this, and I'm sure that God will get in touch sooner or later. So as I look back over the last twenty years, I am truly amazed at the places I've been, the people that I have met, the sights I have seen, the situations that have been overcome, what's been achieved and the lives that have been changed (including my own).

I can still remember the time twenty years ago that I sat by my bed and asked the good Lord to use me. Wow, what a response! Little did I realise. But I am so grateful. It's been an amazing journey and a wonderful experience. And I praise the good Lord for it.

Time has moved on somewhat since I arrived home from Krizbav. It's now February 2010 and one or two things have happened. These happenings have helped me to make up my mind about my future involvement in mission work. Sylvia has had one or two falls recently and has become quite unsteady on her feet. This has limited her mobility, resulting in her being more dependent on me. I gladly accept this responsibility and now believe that it is right for me to be there for her. I just wouldn't be happy being in Romania and finding out that Sylvia had had another fall and I wasn't there to help.

Having found a peace about this, and after being informed by Florin that the final touches had been applied to the dwelling in

Krizbav, I now feel it right to say that my last trip to Romania, was indeed, my last trip. Having written letters of thanks to all the good people who have supported me over these many years and explained the reasons why, many of these people have said that I have made the right decision. I feel good about that, plus the fact that soon I will soon be celebrating my 77th birthday. With this episode of my life completed, I now once again ask the question,

"What now Lord?"